What people are s
Ready, Set, Grow .

MW01000842

God calls every pastor to a specific vision for ministry. Invariably, God's purpose includes making a larger impact than anything that comes from pure determination. To fulfill God's vision, we need to change—we have to stop being driven doers and become catalytic coaches. This creates a powerful culture of multiplying leadership resulting in an equipped, unified, and motivated congregation. Let Pastor Wilson's practical and biblical teaching help you and your church accomplish the vision God has called you to pursue.

—Rob Hoskins
President of OneHope, Pompano Beach, Florida

Some books inform, others encourage, and others provoke thoughts. A few books combine all those and more, leading to genuine transformation. My friend Pastor Scott Wilson's latest book, *Ready, Set, Grow: 3 Conversations That Will Bring Lasting Growth to Your Church,* will change you and your church forever. I don't use those words lightly but with intentional gravity. I would encourage every pastor, church leader, staff member, and volunteer to read this book and discuss each chapter. Then, get ready, get set, and grow more than you ever imagined!

—Dr. Samuel R. Chand
Leadership consultant and author of *Cracking Your Church's Culture Code* (www.samchand.com)

As a pastor for thirty-six years, I've had the privilege to watch Scott Wilson as he has grown in his leadership. In fact, "grown" is the key word because Scott is always growing! He has learned the key to lasting and healthy ministry, which is where most church and organizational growth plans fail because they overlook this key principle of leadership. Here's the point: You cannot grow others if you're not growing yourself. In leadership jargon, we are "the lids" on our organizations, but Scott is showing us how to raise the lid and experience real and lasting growth. I can't think of anyone who is a better example of always raising the lid. He has lived it and learned it, and now, he has taken the time to write about it so the rest of us can get it!

—Gerald Brooks, DD
Grace Outreach Center, Plano, Texas

I heartily endorse Pastor Scott Wilson's new book, *Ready, Set, Grow*. Pastor Scott lives out the principles he shares, and I believe his book will not only inspire you—but more, it will provide clear principles and practices to propel you to the next level in your life and ministry. The book takes you on a fulfilling journey of discovery that helps you break free from the status quo and into the destiny God calls you to.

—Dr. George O. Wood, General Superintendent
The General Council of the Assemblies of God, Springfield, Missouri

I'm a self-professed "people watcher." I've seen church staff and key volunteers struggle to be more than workers in their roles. They wanted to be more and do more, but they didn't know how. Then, when they learned and lived the principles in *Ready, Set, Grow*, everything changed! I witnessed their remarkable transition from workers to multipliers. These principles go far beyond denominational ties or attendance numbers. They are biblical truths that, when applied, create a new culture of dynamic leadership.

—Michael Norman
Lead Pastor, Gracehill Community Church, Dallas, Texas

Pastor Scott's book, *Ready Set, Grow*, was a game-changer for our staff and our church. The principles set us on a trajectory of growth that has continued. This book will change the thinking about staff and leadership development in any church or organization that desires to grow to its full potential. It's one of my favorite leadership books!

—Chad Benson
Pastor, Lifegate Church Burleson, Texas

Scott Wilson gives leaders a real-world view on the value of developing leaders. With clarity, power, and warmth, he outlines the necessary conversations to equip leaders to become multiplying disciples. *Ready, Set, Grow: 3 Conversations That Will Bring Lasting Growth to Your Church* has helped grow our church over 400 people in the last 9 months. If you have a heart to build leaders and expand the kingdom of God, this book should be an essential part of your library—and your leadership model.

—Shayne Walters
Lead Pastor, Mosaic, Cincinnati, Ohio

This was definitely the right book at the right time for me and my church! Pastor Wilson's insights come from personal experience, and his process of leadership development put words and systems to what I was feeling and the direction I knew we needed. This book is a must-read for leaders who are serious about growing their organizations!

—Chris Railey

Lead Pastor, New Community Church, Mesquite, Texas

We all know it's our job to develop leaders, but the task often seems overwhelming. Scott's book takes us through the entire journey to create a comprehensive culture of multiplying leaders. From his principles and stories, you'll learn everything from changing the way you think to putting a plan together to raise up leaders. As someone who has been privileged to see his journey up close, I encourage you to read this book and to apply it to your organization today!

—Wayne Northup

Pastor, Saints Community Church, New Orleans, Louisiana

All of us can become more focused, more effective leaders. *Ready, Set, Grow* is about one team's journey to create a culture of outstanding leadership. It's filled with an incredible combination of inspiration, insights, principles, and practical applications—all designed to help you discover God's process of building leaders who multiply themselves. I've seen God use Scott and these principles. Read it, apply it to your church, and watch God work.

—Dan Hunter

Lead Pastor, Living Church, Mansfield, Texas

Ready, Set, Grow is a book about conversations. Scott Wilson has been my good friend for a decade, and over those years, we have had plenty of conversations. He doesn't pretend to have all the answers, but he's not afraid to ask tough questions. As he has grown, he has become a great leader. When I'm around him, I become a better leader too. Sometimes our conversations are loud, and sometimes they're reflective, but they're always a lot of fun. This book is an invitation for you to join in the conversation.

—Anthony Scoma

Lead Pastor, Southwest Family Fellowship, Austin, Texas

Ready, Set, Grow provides a clear plan for church leaders who want to develop a culture of leadership in their churches—both for the present and for the future. It's a must-read for every church leader, no matter the size of the church.

—John McKinzie
Lead Pastor, Hope Fellowship, Frisco, Texas

Every pastor in the world wants hard working staff . . . but sooner or later, he realizes that's not enough. A team of diligent, determined workers eventually "caps out." We need multiplying leaders, not just workers. If we have a team full of leaders, our ceiling is incredibly high! The secret to any great staff team is having a culture characterized by equipping, multiplying, and inspiring. In *Ready, Set, Grow*, Pastor Scott Wilson shows us the lessons he learned over the years of pastoring his church. I wish I'd learned these lessons sooner! If you're looking to raise the standard of leadership and empower your staff and volunteers, let Pastor Scott be your guide!

—Rob Ketterling
Lead Pastor, River Valley Church, Apple Valley, Minnesota

READY, SET,
GROW

3 Conversations That Will Bring Lasting Growth to Your Church

SCOTT WILSON

Foreword by **JUSTIN LATHROP**

MY HEALTHY CHURCH
Resources for the Spirit-led Church

Published by My Healthy Church
1445 N. Boonville Ave.
Springfield, Missouri 65802

Published in association with The Quadrivium Group—
Orlando, Florida

info@TheQuadriviumGroup.com

Some of the names and roles depicted in this account have been
changed to ensure the anonymity of certain people. However, the
descriptions of events are an accurate portrayal of what took place.

ISBN 978-1-62423-076-9
Printed in the United States of America
16 15 14 13 • 1 2 3 4 5

I would like to dedicate this book to my mentor and friend,
Dr. Samuel R. Chand.

I don't know where I would be without your patient and faithful
guidance. You have been a consistent model of what a life-long learner
looks like. You inspire me to *grow* everyday.

Contents

Acknowledgements

Many people have been instrumental in shaping my life, my leadership, and the principles in this book.

I would like to thank my wife, Jenni, for always being there for me, along with my three sons, Dillon, Hunter, and Dakota. I love you all so much, and I'm so proud of you. Thank you, Jenni, for standing with me through every difficult decision and loving me when it wasn't easy.

I want to thank our church staff and leaders who lived this story with me. The servant leaders of The Oaks have labored tirelessly to see the kingdom of God grow. Thank you for listening to God and following Him no matter what.

I would like to recognize my dear friend Pat Springle who is one of the greatest gifts God has given me in the last five years. Pat is a gifted writer and passionate Christ follower—without him this book wouldn't exist. Thanks, Pat, for helping me get this message out of my heart and into a book. I pray that our work will make a difference in people's lives and cause the church to grow all over the world.

I want to thank my friends, Mark Brewer, Justin Lathrop, and Dan Hunter, for their contribution to the book. You guys were there for every conversation and every application. The people who read this book will learn volumes from your experiences. I love you. I appreciate all you did to grow personally and to pour into others' lives. Thank you for trusting me enough to take this journey with me. All three of you are incredible Multipliers. I stand in awe of how God has used you since that first conversation in 2001.

Finally, I want to thank you for reading this book and for prayerfully considering how it might apply to your life, your leadership, and the leaders at your church.

Ready ... set ... GROW!

Foreword

Forewords are generally written by famous authors, great leaders, celebrities, or experts on the book's topic. I am none of these. My credentials are very different but very real: I'm a living, breathing product of the principles of this book. My life is different because Scott Wilson took our staff team through three incredibly challenging and inspiring conversations. *Ready, Set, Grow* is chock-full of truth illustrating potent lessons for anyone who leads or serves on a team. For me, the principles aren't stale or bland, and they didn't stay inside the dusty covers of a manual. They form the scaffolding of my journey of growth.

I am incredibly privileged to have Scott as my pastor, mentor, business partner, and trusted friend. Scott believes in people. I've lived and served by his side for over eleven years, and one truth stands out: God has given Scott eyes to see the potential in every person who comes near him.

Scott's confidence in God's purpose for people isn't limited to the ones who show tremendous promise. He truly believes in everyone he meets. His enthusiasm, though, isn't superficial. We all know people who are full of "happy talk" and say pleasant things to anyone and everyone. Scott is different. He looks beneath the surface and trusts God to give him spiritual perception. He finds and affirms what God is doing in a person's life. It's an amazing gift—from God to Scott, and then through Scott to everyone in his life. He can be excited about a huge vision, but he never forgets that every individual has hopes, dreams, and a role within that vision. It's an honor to be his friend and partner in ministry.

Actually, this may be "the secret sauce" that has to be added to the principles in this book. The three conversations aren't a rigid formula that guarantees a transition from workers to multipliers. They are a template for rich personal discovery and team dialogue. You can use these principles as a formula to see your team grow as leaders, but if they don't truly believe that you love them and believe in them, the process won't have the same kind of impact it had on our team. Belief in others serves as the great multiplier of leadership development.

For over a decade, I've had the privilege of introducing many people to Scott in our offices at The Oaks. Because of the great things God has done in our church and school (a K–12 charter school), leaders from all over the country and the world come to tour and ask questions. No matter who they are—youth ministry interns or the lead pastors of the largest churches in America—Scott gives them his full, loving attention. He brings them into his office, looks them in the eyes, and asks, "What can I do for you?"

As you read this story of a church staff's three-year journey to grow into multiplying leaders, read it through the lens of belief—belief in God, belief in yourself, and belief in the people on your team. And know this: even if you've never met Scott, I can assure you, he believes in you.

And now, on your mark . . .

Justin Lathrop
Kingdom Connector, www.justinlathrop.com

Growing People, Growing Churches

had been frustrated for a couple of years. I had watched our church
endure several cycles of growth and decline, and I had grown tired
of it. Attempting to find a solution, I went to dozens of conferences
across the country, and I read hundreds of books on leadership—
yes, hundreds. The pattern had become almost comical to our staff.
Here's how they would describe the repeated scenario: "Scott goes to
a conference or reads a new book . . . He tells us he finally has 'the key'
to propel us to the next level of growth . . . We make some changes to
our staff structure, curriculum, worship times, or something else with
the promise that 'This is it!' . . . We may—or may not—see some initial
gains, but in a few weeks or months we're back to the same place we
had been. But just wait, Scott's going to another conference. Maybe this
time he will discover the key to all keys." I'm afraid this assessment is
truer than I would like to admit.

Before I became the pastor of our church, I was on staff as the
youth pastor while my dad was the senior pastor. During that time our
congregation grew from 650 to 900 people several different times, but
we always drifted (or collapsed) back to about 650. We tried everything
imaginable to grow and reach our community more effectively. We

made a lot of good efforts, but for a variety of reasons the growth wasn't sustainable.

As the youth pastor, I was committed to building volunteer leaders. I'm not sure when I fully grasped the goal of producing multiplying leaders who would then have an impact on generations of new leaders coming up behind them, but I poured my life into our volunteers, praying they would reach the full potential of who God made them to be.

Workers, Equippers, and Multipliers

Soon after I became the senior pastor, it dawned on me: every person on our staff team was working at full capacity. They were doing the ministry functions in their areas, but not equipping others to become effective leaders. My father had made a similar observation of the levels of leadership years before: *workers* do the ministry, *equippers* build others who do the work of the ministry, and *multipliers* develop generations of leaders who equip each generation after them.

Our team was a bunch of workers. That's not an indictment; they were fulfilling the expectations we had set for them. However, I realized that unless we changed the way we perceived ourselves and our roles, we would never grow beyond that 650-person mark. That was the limit for a staff team comprised of hard workers. For two years, I wrestled with how to change the culture of our team and shift our identity from workers to equippers, and later to multipliers. Finally, God gave me a plan.

As I evaluated the recent cycles of growth and decline, I realized that we fell back to 650 for a variety of reasons but there was a clear common denominator. On the surface, the cause appeared to be church splits, ethnic migration, and other problems, but underneath all of them was the fact that our leaders weren't building strong networks of relationships, full of vision and passion for God's calling.

We were attracting a lot of people because we had "a good show" on Sunday morning, but our staff members were doing most of the work of the ministry. We didn't challenge enough people, equip enough people, and inspire enough people to own God's calling for our church. To borrow a sports metaphor, we had far too many spectators and not enough players and coaches. Without the glue of love and purpose, fractures and declines were bound to occur. The problem wasn't music or ethnicity or any other reason; the problem was that we didn't have enough competent, multiplying leaders. Our staff had to stop being players on the field; we had to become coaches. We simply had to change.

At this point let me introduce three conversations that ultimately helped us to change. These observations didn't occur as the result of a long staff meeting or a weekend retreat. They emerged from hundreds of conversations with the church team about developing a new culture of leadership development. These three conversations required a three-year transformational process for our church leadership. I knew it wouldn't take long to communicate the concept, but it would take that long to change the culture. These conversations were carefully constructed rockets designed to launch new ways of thinking and acting that would change the course of our team and our church over time.

Here is an overview of the three conversations:

» *Conversation 1:* Becoming models others would want to follow
» *Conversation 2:* Selecting the right people to pour our lives into and equipping them to serve effectively
» *Conversation 3:* Building a third generation of leaders, and in fact, changing the culture so that building multipliers becomes a core value

Heart and Skills

Being a pastor is one of the hardest jobs in the world. We have to blend entrepreneurial talents with a shepherd's heart. Like most pastors, I sometimes have difficulty finding the right blend and balance. Sometimes I'm too tough and at times too soft. I can read books and listen to great speakers, but I always go back to the primary model of leadership, Jesus Christ. Jesus never backed away from calling His followers to the highest standards: lay down your life, deny yourself, serve with pure motives, love God with all your heart, love your neighbor as yourself. He challenges us to give, love, and serve with everything we've got, not because we'll get all kinds of blessings but because God is so magnificent He deserves everything we have.

When Jesus says, "Follow me," He's looking for people who are willing to die to honor Him, not those who give a halfway effort and then come up with excuses. But in addition to His toughness and high expectations, He has a heart of tender compassion. He reached out to touch lepers, welcomed anyone who was humble enough to admit their need for Him, and showed compassion to prostitutes, tax gatherers, and other outcasts. He even reached out countless times to the religious elite who eventually had Him killed. Never before, or since, has anyone been so tough and so tender. Jesus is our example as we lead our staff teams and the example for our staff members who lead their ministry teams. It's inappropriate for us to ask people for anything less, and it's wrong for us to model anything less in our relationships with them.

To be effective, leaders need both heart and skills. Either is insufficient without the other. We have to blend a radical commitment to advance the kingdom of God with the tender affection of a "nursing mother" caring for her children. Vision alone makes us harsh. Compassion alone leaves us weak. Both are essential to good and godly leadership. The stakes are too high for leaders to do only what comes naturally to them. We need to do whatever it takes to follow the example of Christ.

King David led his "mighty men" as one of the most gifted leaders of all time. At that point in his life, he was a glowing example of both tenacity and tenderness. The psalmists reflected on David's leadership:

"He chose David his servant
and took him from the sheep pens;
from tending the sheep he brought him
to be the shepherd of his people Jacob,
of Israel his inheritance.
And David shepherded them with integrity of heart;
with skillful hands he led them" (Ps. 78:70–72).

No one said it would be easy. Leading people with the heart of Christ is a most demanding and yet a most rewarding way to live. Yes, we may have leadership gifts and talents we use in our work, but we always have to look into our hearts to see if our motives are pure. The reason we do things is important.

Paul described his purpose in his letter to the Christians in Colosse: "We proclaim him, admonishing and teaching everyone with all wisdom, so that we may present everyone perfect in Christ. To this end I labor, struggling with all his energy, which so powerfully works in me" (Col. 1:28–29).

Church leadership is not about winning a popularity contest, being known as the coolest pastor in the area, or having people's heads turn when they see us at the ballgame. It's about two things: the eternal destiny of people's souls, and even more, about honoring the One who paid the ultimate price for us. He deserves nothing less than all my heart, all my mind, and all my strength. Jesus calls us to the greatest cause the world has ever known, to the greatest sacrifice of laying down our lives, and He calls us to do it all out of an overflowing heart of tender compassion. That is the starting point of modeling a lifestyle of godly leadership.

Vision and Compassion

Every leader has to wrestle with the tension between what is urgent and what is important. In many cases, it seems urgent to do the work ourselves instead of taking the time to prepare others and then delegate responsibility to them. We can do it quicker than they can, we don't have to spend our time explaining and overseeing, and we can probably do it better anyway. But making decisions based on convenience and urgency short-circuits what is a more important role of leadership: equipping people to take responsibility and multiplying themselves into others' lives.

Transforming the roles of staff from workers to multipliers is a culture shift. It doesn't happen because people read a book or hear a great message. The way people think about themselves and their roles has been reinforced by years of conversations and habits. Real change in one's sense of identity and calling takes time, effort, and patience, but the results are incredibly worthwhile.

I've known pastors over the years who were suspicious of anyone who talked boldly about vision and growing their churches. Some of them grumbled, "Those 'visionaries' are just building their own kingdoms. They don't care about God, and they don't care about people. They're just using people to make themselves more successful." In many cases they're right. Some pastors certainly want to build a huge church for selfish reasons, but it's a big mistake to assume that we know the motives of another leader's heart. I know some incredible visionaries who have been captured by the love of Christ. They trust God for great things—not for their glory, but for His.

Jesus called His followers to give their lives for Him. He still does. Certainly, we want to reinforce the love of God to our staff members, but if we truly love them, we'll point them to Christ and help them walk with Him in boldness and strength. We want them to find fulfillment in their leadership, and the only way that can happen is for them to be moved in the depths of their hearts by God's high calling and deep compassion. We do them a disservice if we call them to anything less.

The most compassionate thing we can do for staff members is to help them become all God wants them to be. Our attitudes, though, need not be fierce and demanding. We should be their biggest cheerleaders as we help them reach higher and farther than ever before! It's not kind, compassionate, or loving to lower the bar to let them "just get by." Turning workers into multipliers will be their greatest thrill and a real joy for us. Some leaders I've known who had problems with a high calling and a big vision didn't want to face their own lethargy. It was more comfortable to remain a "nice pastor" instead of leading people to change the culture with vision, passion, and hard work.

I'm known as a visionary, but my heart's desire isn't to grow a church. I would rather grow *people* and help them reach their God-inspired potential. I don't want my staff members to work hard to fulfill my vision—*they* are my vision! Everything I do is designed to push and pull our staff to follow Christ with their whole hearts and make the biggest impact they can make for His kingdom. The biggest impact occurs when leaders produce more leaders who produce even more leaders for generations to come.

A Look at Motives

As you begin this book and consider implementing the three conversations, take a hard look at your motives. All of us have mixed motives. Some mix desire to please God with fear of disapproval, and some of us are tainted by the thirst for power. We shouldn't be surprised when the Holy Spirit shines His light on the dark places in our hearts. But when He does, we need to repent, thank God for His forgiveness, and choose His path. It's important to be ruthlessly honest with God about our deepest desires. We may teach what we know, but we reproduce who we are. All of us are in the long, slow, painful process of allowing God to change who we are. If we don't address impure and destructive motives in our own hearts, we will model those selfish desires to the people around us.

Jesus told the religious leaders, "Woe to you, teachers of the law and Pharisees, you hypocrites! You travel over land and sea to win a single convert, and when he becomes one, you make him twice as much a son of hell as you are" (Matt. 23:15). That's modeling and multiplication, but the wrong kind!

We need to think hard about what motivates us to do everything we do. If we're seeking power and approval, we might impress people at a distance, but those who hang out with us every day clearly see the truth—and they're repulsed. Whenever I get carried away with how great my vision is or how popular I'm becoming (or if I'm afraid of failing and being rejected), I remember Christ gave Himself for me. It's the great inversion: He was fabulously rich living in heaven, but He stepped out of glory to earth to die a criminal's death for me and you. He became poor to make us rich beyond our wildest imaginations—not in money or possessions (though He gives enough of those, too), but in mercy, love, and purpose.

Is Christ worthy of my affection? Is there anything about Him that calls forth my deepest ambition to please Him and Him alone? The writer to the Hebrews said it well: "Let us fix our eyes on Jesus, the author and perfecter of our faith, who for the joy set before him endured the cross, scorning its shame, and sat down at the right hand of the throne of God. Consider him who endured such opposition from sinful men, so that you will not grow weary and lose heart" (Heb. 12:2–3).

I need to "consider Him" frequently to keep my heart fresh and flooded with His mercy. When I reflect more deeply on who Jesus is and what He has done for me, I'm overwhelmed that He wants to use me as a channel of His grace to turn people from hell to heaven and help them take steps to become all God wants them to be. What a thrill!

At one point while I was a youth pastor, my motives were rotten. I was driven to produce the biggest, best ministry anywhere, and I used people to accomplish what I wanted. Of course, I cloaked my motives in talk about God's will and reaching the lost, but honestly, it was all about me. I got angry with people when they didn't contribute enough to my program. I viewed them as the machinery to crank out my ministry. Do you think they could tell? Of course they could. We lived in a tug of war as I struggled to control them and they resisted my leadership.

For a long time I complained angrily to God, "What's wrong with these people?" God's answer was different than I expected. I hoped He would fix them, but He planned to fix me. One night during a prayer meeting at a retreat, He led me to a passage in Ezekiel. God spoke through the prophet. Here's what He said:

> "Son of man, prophesy against the shepherds of Israel; prophesy
> and say to them: 'This is what the Sovereign LORD says: Woe
> to the shepherds of Israel who only take care of themselves!

Should not shepherds take care of the flock? You eat the curds, clothe yourselves with the wool and slaughter the choice animals, but you do not take care of the flock. You have not strengthened the weak or healed the sick or bound up the injured. You have not brought back the strays or searched for the lost. You have ruled them harshly and brutally. So they were scattered because there was no shepherd, and when they were scattered they became food for all the wild animals. My sheep wandered over all the mountains and on every high hill. They were scattered over the whole earth, and no one searched or looked for them'" (Ezek. 34:2–6).

It was as if someone had hit my head with a sledgehammer. Every word was true of me, but God wasn't through. He added,

"I am against the shepherds and will hold them accountable for my flock. I will remove them from tending the flock so that the shepherds can no longer feed themselves. I will rescue my flock from their mouths, and it will no longer be food for them" (Ezek. 34:10).

God's Spirit spoke as plainly to my heart as a man speaks to a friend, "If you don't change, I'm taking you out. These aren't *your* people. They're *My* people. I've put you there to watch over them, not to use them. If you love them and care for them, I'll reward you. You don't have to worry about that. But if you keep using them to build your own kingdom to make you look good, I'll remove you from ministry. You see yourself as 'a general in God's army,' but you're acting like a pimp, using people under the guise of love. This, son, must change. I want someone who is a shepherd of My flock, someone who loves Me enough and loves them enough to lay down his life for them. Do you understand?"

I fell to my knees and wept. I offered no excuses. There was no debate. Everything God had said through Ezekiel to the wicked shepherds of Israel was true of me, and I knew it. I asked God, "What do I do now? I'm willing to do anything."

The next morning I was scheduled to speak to the group at the retreat, but my topic had changed. I read the passage from Ezekiel and told them, "This passage was written to me and about me. I've been using you, not loving you." Many people in the room began to cry as I continued, "I wanted to follow God and lead people, but somehow, I got off track. I've used you. I've gotten mad at you. I'm so sorry. Will you forgive me?" I paused for a second to compose myself, and then I said, "I've asked Mark to play some soft music. I'm going to be at the front. If you'll come down, I'd like to ask you individually to forgive me. I want to pray for you and wash your feet."

I stepped away from the lectern and picked up a bowl of water and a towel. Person after person came to spend a few minutes with me. They cried and I cried. I asked each one to forgive me. I prayed for them and washed their feet. For three hours, they kept coming. They had felt misused and unappreciated so long that they didn't seem to mind waiting for healing to begin.

I've never forgotten the pain and glory of that moment. It was one of the most gut-wrenching times of my life because God showed up and pointed out my deepest sins, but it was glorious because He forgave me and began to change me in the deepest recesses of my heart. The faces of those people at the retreat are etched in my mind. The pain I had caused would still haunt me if they harbored bitterness toward me, but they were gracious and forgave me. Their grace to me is something I will never take for granted. I'll treasure it the rest of my life.

My habit of relating to others as a military general took some time to change, but I gave them permission to speak truth to me about how I was coming across—and they did. I was motivated more than ever to change my behavior, my attitude, and the way I communicated with people. I wanted them to know, so I told them often, that I wanted them to delight in the love of God. When I talked about obedience, it was for their good and God's glory, not to manipulate or control them. Gradually, we all changed. I'll never be the same. I could never have led our staff team as a senior pastor until God purged me of the sin of pride and manipulation. This humbling experience set the stage for the three conversations.

Jesus, as John tells us in his Gospel, was full of grace and truth. Both of those qualities should be present in our leadership as well—whether we oversee a veteran staff of hundreds or a fledgling group of volunteers. As we call people to give everything they have for Christ, they need to be convinced that we love them and care more about them than their performance. It's important to examine our motives at the outset of this journey and throughout the years of changing the culture. I had to take an honest look at my heart countless times during the process, but I could always recall the day God corrected me. It was the benchmark of God's grace and truth in my life and my leadership.

My Hope for You

I'm so excited about all the great things God did in our staff team over three years! The three conversations revolutionized our expectations, the level of our leadership, and our hearts. We became better leaders because we went through this process, and even more importantly, we became better people. Success is not about numbers or church growth or leadership principles. This book is about finding and following God's design to pour His grace into more people. That's what leadership multiplication is all about. Along the way I learned some important lessons about myself. Our team grew in every way, and in fact, at one point the success almost shattered our team and ruined all we had seen God do. (We'll get to that later.)

The principles in this book are adaptable. They are based on biblical concepts of equipping and multiplying, so they apply to churches of every size, from church plants to mega-churches, from a bi-vocational pastor with a few volunteers to those with teams of paid staff in every department.

As you begin the journey, examine your motives to see why you do what you do—whether you're the senior pastor or a member of the staff team, motives count. I hope God doesn't have to speak as strongly to you as He did to me, but if He does, listen.

Don't try to implement a multiplication strategy unless your life is worth emulating. Your people will pray like you pray, love like you love, and speak truth like you speak truth. They will disciple others the way you disciple them. So challenge people boldly to a higher calling and a strategy of multiplying themselves in the lives of others, but first (and always) ensure that God's calling and grace is deep in your heart. You have to own it before you can give it away.

When you chart your course and set sail, expect some headwinds. People will push back for any number of reasons. They may accuse you of being too harsh, even when you let them set their own goals. They may wonder about your motives, even though you're honest about having mixed motives and you express your desire to please God above all else. When people push back, don't overreact. Some people are lazy and some are rebellious, but don't impulsively use such labels. A lot of people resist change because they want to understand everything before taking that first step. Others simply prefer the security of the known to the uncertainties of the unknown. And even if you're crystal clear in your direction and eager to move ahead, don't be surprised when some people ask innumerable questions or drag their feet. Jesus was the perfect leader, and He had the Father's plan. He even got to select His staff team . . . and look at the resistance He encountered!

This book has three sections, each with three chapters. Each section begins with a conversation followed by what happened that year and the lessons I learned. I describe exactly what we did with our team, and I also explain, in retrospect, what I think we should have done differently. I hope you catch the heart of the strategy in each conversation. If you do, you can adapt the specifics to fit your situation and your team.

In this book I share my philosophy of leadership development, and of course, I present the strategy and plans from my point of view. At the end of each section I include comments from others on my team as they heard these three conversations and implemented the plans. The training model in this book isn't a top-down mandate to read books and listen to talks—it's about shepherding people on a team and helping them become mature, strong, loving multipliers. So if you're considering this training model, don't focus on extrinsic behavior and miss the intrinsic motivation; don't try to implement a strict formula to the exclusion of the underlying principles. The people who were on our staff team during those three years will provide a clear picture of the heart and soul of the entire process.

At the end of the first section, Mark Brewer shares his experiences. Mark was our worship leader at the time, and he currently serves as our Executive Pastor of Ministries. Later Dan Hunter gives his insights about the second conversation. Dan was our student pastor at the time, and he currently serves as Lead Pastor at Living Church in Mansfield, Texas. The third section concludes with comments from Justin Lathrop. When we began these three years of training, Justin was new to our team as the pastor of our young adults, but he jumped in with both feet. During the third year, God used the process of discovery to launch Justin into a new phase of his career. I hope you benefit from the willingness of these three men to share their enthusiasm and lessons learned, as well as their fears and doubts.

I have also included some questions at the end of each chapter to help you think more deeply and to devise your own implementation plan. I encourage you and your team to read the whole book to see where it's going, and then come back to discuss each chapter over a period of weeks or months. Then, when you're ready, it will be time to blast off! May you have a great ride!

Think about it . . .

1. What is your purpose for picking up this book? What do you hope to get out of it?

2. Why is an examination of motives essential when we begin to implement a new leadership strategy?

3. If you were completely honest about your leadership style, which are you: a shepherd or a general?

Chapter 1

The First Conversation: Get Ready

Our staff members came into my office that morning laughing and kidding around with each other as they always had. As usual, our relationships were warm and positive. We enjoyed hanging out with each other, and it showed. They were expecting our usual staff meeting—none of them knew what was coming.

There were eight of us: Justin was in charge of young adults; Dave coordinated the children's ministry; Dan led the student ministry; Joel was our director of media arts; Mark was our worship leader; Richard led the senior adults; Brittany was the director of our women's ministry; and I had been the senior pastor for a couple of years. I had been preparing for this meeting for weeks, but I hadn't dropped any clues about what was going to happen. I wanted our first conversation to be fresh—even shocking.

After the banter died down, I began by reviewing the recent history of the church. "Most of you were here two years ago when we grew from about 650 people to 900 in the fall. Do you remember that?" Everybody smiled and nodded. "Do you remember what our numbers were by that Christmas?"

"Yeah," Dave smiled knowingly. "We tanked."

"We were back down to about 600 to 650 again, weren't we?" I replied. "That spring, we pulled out all the stops and invited everybody in town to a sermon series, and we grew up to about 900 again. Do you remember what happened next?"

Mark shook his head: "Two hundred and fifty people left to join another church up the road."

I nodded, "And the same thing happened the next year. We grew to about 900, and then a bunch of people left, but not to go to another church. They just drifted away because we lost momentum."

I let this sink in for a few seconds, and then I told them, "The meeting today is really important. It's huge. I want to ask a question and I want you to think about it before you answer. How many people—what size church—do you think this staff team can lead?"

Mark didn't take long to answer: "A thousand people."

After a brief pause, others jumped in: "Twelve hundred." "Nine hundred."

Dan was a bit more ambitious. "Fifteen hundred. I know a staff in Dallas that isn't as sharp as ours, and they have over twelve hundred, so we should be able to do at least that."

When everyone who wanted to speculate had spoken, I announced: "Fine. I'm going to tell you the accurate number."

Justin shook his head in mock disgust. "Well, great. Why didn't you just tell us what you thought from the beginning?"

"Because I wanted to know what you were thinking. That's important." I took a deep breath, and I continued, "I'll tell you exactly what size church this staff team can lead. I'm absolutely sure of my number because I have rock solid proof." I had their attention now. "This staff team can lead 650 people."

"Why do you say that?" Dave asked.

"Because that's how many people we have right now."

Almost in unison, several of them spoke up, "Yeah, but we can grow!"

I was ready with a carefully prepared answer. I looked into their eyes and responded, "Every time we grow larger, we shrink back to 650. It's like we're a bucket with holes at a certain level." I went to the whiteboard and drew a bucket with holes in it **(Figure 1)**. "We can pour more into it all day long, but it leaks down to the level where the holes are. It's inevitable. That's what happened to us. Not once, not twice, but three times. Even when we have growth, we don't have the capacity to retain it, much less grow even more. That's our limit: 650."

Figure 1

Breaking 1,000

The looks on their faces at that moment ranged from confusion to insight to a trace of anger. At least nobody looked bored. I told them, "I have an announcement. We're going to break one thousand, and this time, we're not going back down to 650. You can count on it. For that to happen, though, something has to change. It's not going to happen by magic, and it's not going to happen because we offer one more cool program that attracts a lot of people for a while. As of today, we're starting something new that's going to change us. One year from now, this staff will be different. Either each of you will have changed to improve your skills and capacity for ministry, or I'll find people with those characteristics to replace you. It's going to happen one way or the other. Either you'll change, or you'll be replaced. In other words, you've got to grow, or you'll have to go."

The silence in the room was so complete I could almost hear my heart beating. Not a word, not a movement, and barely a breath. Before they could argue with me, I kept going, hoping to allay their fears. "Let me show you how this is going to work." On the whiteboard, I drew a basketball goal like those on a pole in a driveway. Next to the net, I wrote "1,000" **(Figure 2)**. I told them, "The goal is clear. We're going to reach 1,000 people on a normal Sunday—not on Easter or Christmas, but in the middle of February or June or October."

I had planned my next statement for a week or so: "If you can't dunk the ball, you can't stay on our staff." I could see their discomfort rising, so I asked the question they were all secretly thinking. "But that wouldn't be fair, would it? None of us can dunk a basketball. I know, because I've played with all of you. And you know *I* can't do it. One of you might say, 'I could dunk if you made it an eight-foot goal.' But here's the deal: we're not going to lower the goal to accommodate our current

Figure 2

ability. That's not going to happen. I believe God has called me as the
pastor, and our church as His body in this community, to reach more
people with the gospel. Right now, I'm convinced that we're not doing
all we can do to fulfill God's calling. That's what this meeting is about.
It's not about the number 1,000. That's just an arbitrary figure. And I'm
not telling you that we have to get there by a certain date. It's going to
take some time, probably two or three years. But I'm much more interested in the culture we create on our staff. If we learn to build hundreds
of leaders, we'll reach that number."

I waited a few seconds for this explanation to sink in. Dave spoke
for the whole group when he said, with more than a hint of discouragement, "I don't know how to make this happen—no matter how much
time you give us."

Will and Skill

That's the response I was looking for, so I continued. "Here's what I'll do. It's my responsibility as your leader to build stairs so you can climb them and dunk the ball. I drew steps on the whiteboard in front of the basketball goal **(Figure 3)**. Our goal is 1,000 people. That's not going to change, but I'm telling you today that I'll do everything in my power to equip you, help you, support you, and encourage you so that we reach that goal together. I'll build the steps so you can reach the goal, but you have to have two things: the will and the skill to make it happen. I can help you develop your skill, but the will is all yours. If you don't take the steps to dunk the ball, it's because you can't or you won't. Either way, you can't stay."

Figure 3

About half the people in the room were starting to get excited. A couple of them were puzzled because they didn't have all the information they wanted, and one or two were skeptical. Based on the faces of the ones who were hesitant, I suspected they were thinking, *Man, Scott is off his rocker. He must have gone to a leadership conference or listened to a CD or something. Where does he get this stuff?*

Despite my suspicions, I knew most of them would catch on as we kept talking and started developing our plans. I told them, "Let me tell you what I've learned about church staff. There are three kinds of staff members: *workers, equippers,* and *multipliers.*" I wrote those words on the board **(Figure 4)**. (Most of the people in the room were workers, although at that point they probably would have identified themselves as equippers. We would need to raise the bar and redefine excellence over the next couple of years.)

Figure 4

I opened my Bible and said, "In Ephesians, Paul outlines the role of Christian leaders. You know this passage as well as I do. Here's what he wrote in Ephesians 4:11–13: 'It was he who gave some to be apostles, some to be prophets, some to be evangelists, and some to be pastors and teachers, to prepare God's people for works of service, so that the body of Christ may be built up until we all reach unity in the faith and in the knowledge of the Son of God and become mature, attaining to the whole measure of the fullness of Christ.'" I paused for a second, and then asked, "So how are we going to reach the whole measure of the fullness of Christ as a church?"

Dan said, "By getting the people of God to do the work of the ministry."

"That's right," I answered, "And who's supposed to equip them?"

Mark said, "I guess that would be us."

"That's right, *we* are!" I explained, "Workers do the work of ministry, but they don't equip others. Folks, God has called us to be equippers, to pour ourselves into other people, to model spiritual life and help others be effective in serving God. For anybody in Christian leadership, that's a minimum expectation. But I believe God wants us to go a step further, to equip people who will equip people who will equip people."

The lights were coming on in the eyes of my staff. I said, "Let's look at the advice Paul gave Timothy. It's in 2 Timothy 2:1–2: 'You then, my son, be strong in the grace that is in Christ Jesus. And the things you have heard me say in the presence of many witnesses entrust to reliable men who will also be qualified to teach others' (2 Tim. 2:1–2).

Do you see it? Paul told Timothy to be a *multiplier*. Certainly don't settle for being a worker, and don't even settle for being an equipper."

It was time to connect the dots before we went any further. I told them, "Our church is not going to grow and reach our community if it's up to the eight of us trying harder. You already work your tails off. That's not the problem." They seemed to be relieved to hear that. "The only way we're going to reach our goal is by changing who we are, what we model to the people we lead, and how we equip them to lead others."

"So," Justin said slowly, "what exactly does this mean for us?"

"It means this: it's not good enough for those of us in this room to be *workers*. A year from now, this church won't have anybody on pastoral staff who is only a worker. That role doesn't fit with the biblical role of leadership, and practically, it prevents others from being trained and put into effective places to serve. No, we won't have any workers on our staff this time next year. Either you'll become an *equipper*, or we'll find someone who is."

I paused for a few seconds to let this sink in, and then I told them, "And two years from now—you see where this is going, don't you? Two years from now, we won't be paying anybody on our staff who is only an equipper. All of our staff will be *multipliers*. Any questions?"

Only one person was strangely silent through this discussion. Brittany was already doing a great job pouring herself into a team of leaders in the women's ministry, and those leaders were actively discipling other women. Her ministry was so strong that it put the rest of the team to shame, and to be honest, a few of the guys were more than a bit jealous of her success. When others talked glowingly of Brittany and the team of leaders she had assembled, I heard comments like, "Yeah, but she works with people who don't have anything else to do and are available all day every day. The people on my team have to work." Such criticism had a kernel of truth, but the fact is that about half the women on Brittany's leadership team were women who worked and had children at home. She had selected well, devoted herself to building those women, and equipped them to multiply themselves in the lives of others. She had been silent during our discussions because she was probably thinking, *What took these guys so long?* But she didn't say it, and she didn't smirk. She was gracious to the guys who could learn a lot from her.

Don't Just Add—Multiply!

Richard was thinking hard. I knew something good was coming, and then he said, "Scott, the Ephesians passage says our role is to 'equip the saints for the work of ministry.' I get that, but I'm not sure it's right to ask us to be multipliers, and to tie our jobs to that goal. Help me understand what you're thinking."

"Great point, Richard. Let me put it another way. The Great Commission challenges us to make disciples of all nations. For that to happen, there has to be some significant leadership development. The Ephesians passage applies to all leaders. It directs every Christian leader to equip people to serve God and to make a difference in the lives of others." Richard wasn't sure where I was going, so I asked him, "Do you have leaders in the senior adult ministry?"

"Yes, I have teachers of the Sunday school classes."

"Do they have teams to shepherd the people in the classes?"

"Well," Richard thought for a second. "Some do and some don't."

"Suppose for a moment they all do. It then becomes the role of the Sunday school teachers to equip those on their teams to care for the people in the classes, right?"

He was nodding now.

"And your role is to equip the equippers. I call a person in that role a multiplier. We can call it a 'leader of leaders' or anything else that you want, but the point is that an organization can only grow to the point where leadership development stops. That is the problem of stagnation. It's a roadblock. It creates holes in the bucket that prevent further growth."

Others were on board with this idea now, but I wasn't through. "I'm not asking you to be anything or do anything God doesn't want for you. I'm only trying to put handles on God's calling. We aren't going to arrive where God wants us to go by straining more, working more hours, or finding a magic program. It's all about developing leaders who will develop more leaders. It's not enough to be a disciple, and we're not going to reach the world if we only learn to disciple others. We have to become leaders who dis-

> We have to become leaders who disciple disciplers. Wherever that process stops, we stop growing. But I don't think we ever have to stop.

ciple disciplers. Wherever that process stops, we stop growing. But I don't think we ever have to stop. That's what's so exciting!"

I could see from the expression on Mark's face that he wasn't sure how this new concept applied to his responsibility of leading worship. I asked, "Mark, what do you think about all of this?"

He began to reply in his usual, reflective way. "I really like the vision and the goal, and I think the strategy of equipping people to become multipliers is cool, but I'm not sure how it applies to me. The rest of the people on this team are in roles of spiritual leadership. I'm not."

I told him, "You raise a very interesting point." Then I asked, "Do you ever feel that some of your singers or musicians feel stressed because they're doing too much?"

He laughed. "You know the answer to that. Yeah, of course. Some of our people sing or play almost every Sunday."

"As we grow, do you think you might need more people to help?"

"We need them now. If we grow and don't find more people to help, my people will crater."

"And is it possible that you might need to organize them so that you have different bands, different groups of singers, and maybe a choir for certain occasions?"

Mark's eyes lit up. "Yes, I see what you mean." He paused a second, and then he observed, "So . . . the strategy of equipping and multiplying doesn't just apply to pastoral leadership. It works in every area of the church."

"Exactly. But we'll have to tailor the specifics to fit each area."

Step One: Model

I had done most of the talking up to this point, and now I wanted to shift gears and have a group discussion. My staff members were realizing this wasn't a plan that I was going to forget before we met again the next week or in a few months. They could tell that I was 100 percent committed to this vision, but we had only outlined the bare bones of the strategy. It was time to get more specific. I introduced the next part of our meeting by telling them, "Everything in leadership development begins with modeling. If people don't see it in you, they won't do it themselves. It's that simple. It's not good enough to have great training seminars or flow charts or diagrams. Passion and compassion need to seep out of every pore of our lives."

They had heard me talk dozens of times about the importance of modeling, so this wasn't anything new. They wondered, though, how the concept applied to our new goal and the challenge of learning to be equippers. I explained, "We can't take people where *we* haven't been. We can't pour into people if we're not full and overflowing. So this first year, our task is to get filled up so that we burst with spiritual vitality, leadership insights, passion for Christ, and love for the people in our lives! Nothing else, and nothing less. The first year, our goal is filling our hearts. Then we can pray for God's grace to fill us, become contagious, and spread into an epidemic that sweeps across this community!" (I may have shifted from talking to preaching with that last comment, but at least the group understood what I meant.)

I told them, "I've been talking a lot, and now I want to throw the discussion open to you. I want you to consider what it will take to be filled with these qualities. What can we commit to as a staff team? And I want you to project what we will model for the people on our ministry teams. Imagine what kind of spouses, parents, and neighbors we will be. Think of the difference it will make in our prayer lives, our private worship, our corporate worship, and every aspect of our church life. What can we do to fill our lives so that we become great models? Whatever we decide to do, we're going to do it together. We're going to make a covenant among ourselves and with God."

Dave spoke first. "I think we can go to conferences. I've always benefited from them."

Dan said, "Scott, you're always telling us stuff you get out of reading books. Maybe we could read some great books and talk about them."

Brittany added, "I've been listening to podcasts that are fantastic, and some webinars that are great, too."

We batted around a few other ideas, but we soon settled on books and CDs or podcasts as the main sources of input for our team. I tried to bring us to a conclusion, "Okay, how many and what kinds of books and CDs are we going to commit to?"

Justin asked me, "How many books do you read? How many CDs do you listen to?"

"I probably read a book a week, and I listen to a CD every day on the road to and from home."

I could tell my answer freaked them out. Justin moaned, "Well, great, but that's you. Maybe we could do something more reasonable."

My comment, though, had a significant benefit: it let the others know I was committed to staying ahead of them. I had to model the things I was asking them to do. As their leader, I had to do more than they were doing.

> I had to model the things I was asking them to do. As their leader, I had to do more than they were doing.

I quickly assured them, "Hey, I'm not going to tell you what our commitment needs to be. That's a group decision. Talk about it, negotiate with one another, and come to a consensus. Remember, though, that you need to prepare yourself so you're able to reach your goal. Don't set the goal too high or you'll get discouraged, but don't make it too low or you won't be equipped. It's your call."

A lively discussion followed about what the numbers should be. One person lobbied for the team to keep up with me, but he was shot down pretty quickly. The suggested number of books ranged between twenty-five and forty, but they eventually settled on thirty-six. (I have no idea where the number came from, but it was theirs, and they owned it.) They all had access to all kinds of CDs and podcasts, so they decided on two a week: 104 during the year.

Richard asked, "Scott, how many are you committing to? Are you with us, 36 and 104?"

"I'm planning on staying with my current plan for the books: fifty-two this year. I'm not sure how many messages I will listen to. It might not be five a week. I'll tell you what: I'll commit to three a week. That's 156."

Then I asked, "What kinds of books are you going to read? What are the topics of the CDs, podcasts, and other things you'll listen to and watch?"

Dave shrugged, "Well, leadership, I guess."

"Yeah, that's part of it, but I want this material to fill your souls, not just your minds. Pick material on spiritual formation, family life, ministry areas, understanding people, prayer, and all kinds of things."

"You mean, we can pick anything we want to?" Richard asked.

"Well, not *anything*. Romance novels and horror stories are out. No *Twilight*, and no *Left Behind*." They laughed. "But in the areas of spiritual life and leadership, it's wide open."

The Plan

I hadn't had time to think through our selection of books, so at the moment I was winging it. I proposed, "Let's do this. I'll pick twelve books for us to read and study together. We'll cover one a month in staff meetings so that we're all on the same page. The other book choices will be up to you." Hearing no objection, I continued. "By this time next week, I want you to have a list of the twenty-four books you want to read. I'll pick the twelve we'll study as a team. Is that good for you?"

They seemed to like that plan. As my gaze shifted from person to person, I realized that some of them were avid readers, but others seldom read anything but the sports section of the paper. I wanted to acknowledge their differences while we were making a covenant together, so I told them, "Some of you are going to do much more than what we've agreed to today, and some of you will have to try really hard to meet these goals. That's why I wanted you to come up with the numbers on your own. I don't want you to get to the middle of the year and blame me for pushing you too hard. It's no big deal for Richard to read thirty-six books. He probably read that many in the past month!"

They all knew that Richard never watched television, and he read all the time, but they also knew my statement was a bit of hyperbole. Richard chuckled, "Not quite. Maybe only thirty-four or thirty-five."

Mark had been on board up to this point, but now had a puzzled expression on his face. I said, "Mark, something's bothering you. What is it? Let's talk about it."

"What if somebody just reads all the books, listens to the CDs, looks at videos online, and participates in seminars on the web, but it's all just checking off boxes? What good is that going to do?"

I was thrilled that he asked that question. I told him, "Man, you're right on target, Mark. It's absolutely worthless if we just go through the motions to finish the books and messages as quickly as possible. That's not the goal at all. The reason we're doing this is to feed our souls. When somebody gets near us, I want them to smell our passion for God and our excitement about seeing people grow. When somebody bumps into us, I want God's love and Christ's commitment to reach the world to spill out of us. That's the purpose of this covenant."

> I can't be the person God wants me to be if I'm not exposing my heart to gifted teachers who challenge me to love more and lead better.

Yeah, yeah, I had started preaching again. I stopped for a second to collect my thoughts, and then reemphasized, "The goal of 1,000 people is arbitrary, and the timeline is flexible. What's not negotiable is our commitment to become the kind of people others will follow—people they can't wait to hang out with. If we complete our assignments without filling our souls, we're just wasting our time. The reason I read and listen to CDs is that I need—I *desperately* need—to be inspired and challenged by the best and brightest people in God's kingdom. I can't be the person God wants me to be if I'm not exposing my heart to gifted teachers who challenge me to love more and lead better."

Mark smiled, "Okay. I get it." Everybody laughed. They always laugh (or at least smile) when I get excited and start preaching in staff meetings. I'm not offended. I would react the same way.

Let's Get Motivated

I continued to define the vision for the coming year. "I believe God wants us to be a staff that helps people reach their full, God-given potential. That won't happen by each of you making a commitment to me. We need to pull for each other, to kick each other in the butt when we need it, and to celebrate like crazy when we see God using us to build leaders in our ministries. Your commitment isn't to the church or to me; it's to God and to the whole team. Do you get that?"

"Yeah, that's cool," Justin spoke for the group.

"And as motivation, I want to give you dual encouragement, a carrot and a stick. A year from today, I'm going to ask you to bring to staff meeting a list of the thirty-six books you read and the 104 messages you listened to or videos you watched. When you hand that to me, I'm going to give you a check for $500, and then we're going to take the rest of the day off to go play golf, watch a movie, go bowling—whatever you want to do—and then go out to a really nice dinner with our spouses. Cool, huh?"

I had hoped this would inspire them, but Dave didn't miss a beat: "And the stick?"

"If you come to that meeting without hitting those goals, you won't get a check, and you won't be going with us to celebrate that day. And one more thing: you and I will have a private meeting. I will give you ten minutes to explain to me why you should stay on our staff team."

Joel's eyes got big. "You're serious." It was more of a question than a comment.

"Absolutely serious. Look, if we make this commitment to each other and somebody doesn't fulfill it, he's either lazy or a liar. You either don't want to fulfill your commitments, or you can't. Those are huge character issues for a spiritual leader." I was a bit incredulous that Joel could have any doubts about my sincerity after I had poured out my heart and outlined the plan to them for the past hour, but now I was sure he understood.

Commitment Time

Dave suddenly realized that all those books and CDs were going to cost some money. He asked, "Scott, is the church going to pay for all this stuff we're going to read and listen to?"

To be honest, I hadn't thought about that. I had to wing my answer again. "Great question, Dave. How about this? The church will pay for the twelve we're going to study together, and you'll be responsible to get the others. But you know the church has a huge library of books and CDs on leadership by Maxwell, Hybels, and other top Christian leaders. You can check those out anytime you want to. One of you can buy a book and several of you can share it. You can buy used books online that are really cheap. And you can download a lot of the audio messages for free. With a little planning, you may not have to spend a penny on any of this stuff. If you do, then the $500 will reimburse you for your expenses. How's that?"

Dave nodded, and as I looked around the room, the others were nodding too. (Dodged that bullet.)

As I looked around the room it appeared that everyone was on board, but I wanted each person's verbal commitment. I said, "Okay, are you willing to trust God together, to reach this goal, to commit to the plan of thirty-six books and 104 messages?" I looked at each one in turn.

"Justin, are you in?"

"Yes."

"Mark, are you with me?"

"I'm with you."

"Dave?"

"I guess so."

I was surprised by his answer. "What do you mean, 'I guess so?'"

He averted eye contact as he replied, "I've read so many books on spiritual life and leadership." He paused for a second, and then he looked at me and said, "Don't get me wrong. I'm in, but I'm not excited about it."

I nodded, "I understand. Will you stay a little while after we meet? I want us to look at books on my shelf to see if there are any that interest you."

"Cool."

"Joel, how about you?"

"No problem."

"Dan?"

"I'm excited! This is exactly what we need."

"Richard, what do you think?"

"Sign me up, captain."

"Britt, are you in?"

"Absolutely!" She could hardly contain her excitement.

I responded, "Fantastic! I believe this is a turning point in the life of our church, our staff team, and for each of us individually." I then prayed that God would lead us and use the books and messages to fill our hearts and transform our lives, and that in return we would model the life and passion of Christ in every corner of our church and the community.

"See you next week," I told them as they left the meeting. "Don't forget to bring a list of the books and CDs you're planning to use this next year. I'll bring the list of twelve I'm picking for us to study together."

When the last one left the room, I took a deep breath. *Good start,* I said to myself.

Mark's Initial Response

**Mark Brewer was our worship leader when we
began the first conversation. He now serves as the
Executive Pastor of Ministries at The Oaks.**

When Scott introduced the strategy of turning workers into multipliers, I wasn't surprised at all. Whenever he went to a conference or read a new book, he came to our staff meetings with the latest and greatest strategy that was "going to change everything." It wasn't just Scott who got excited about new ideas. Most of the people on our team were learners. We were always looking for ways to reach more people and minister more effectively.

As Scott challenged us to consider how many people our current staff team could handle, it was sobering. We all wanted to think of ourselves as sharp and skilled, and we had plenty of excuses why our numbers had declined from about 900 back to 650 several times. But that morning, Scott wasn't into excuses. He said the pattern spoke volumes. Our team could effectively lead only 650 people. That was the level where our bucket had holes. At that moment, I knew Scott was right on target. His logic was impeccable, but I felt discouraged. Like everyone else on our team, I had been trying hard. We had been giving God and the church everything we had, but we were stuck. I didn't know how to break out of the stagnant pattern we had fallen into, but I was ready to hear Scott's solution.

When Scott talked about moving from workers to equippers to multipliers, the concepts weren't new. We had talked about Jethro and Moses, 2 Timothy 2:2, and other passages. We had read books and articles, and had been to countless conferences on leadership. But there was a problem: I already saw myself as an equipper, even though I was much more of a worker. I could speak the language of multiplication, but my actions didn't match my words. I remember looking around the room and thinking, *Maybe I'm not a multiplier yet, but I know who the workers are on our team. They'd better get their act together!* I had a lot to learn.

It was tremendously important that Scott engaged us in negotiating the requirements of reading books and listening to messages. To be honest, it was a new day for him and for us. Prior to that morning he had given us plenty of motivations along with directives, but in this conversation, he asked us to own the process of making the decisions about the books and messages. When we settled on the numbers, I immediately realized there would be a cost involved. I would have to rearrange my schedule to fit in the reading and listening. I was excited, though, because we were doing it as a team.

Think about it . . .

1. What kind of preparation do you think Scott did for this meeting?

2. What did he do well? What might he have done differently?

3. If you had been in the room that day, how would you have responded at different points in the conversation? For example:

   » The concept of the bucket with holes in it

   » The vision and the goal of 1,000 people

   » The three kinds of staff members

   » The challenge to become good models

   » The plan to read books and listen to messages

4. Which aspects of Scott's strategy and delivery with his staff that day seemed right on target? What (if anything) was over the top?

5. Can you envision yourself having this conversation, either as the pastor or a staff member? Why or why not?

Chapter 2

The Events of the First Year: Progress and Resistance

As I reflected on that confrontational conversation with my staff, I was excited about their response to our new vision and direction. They all said they were in! To be honest, I hadn't thought through how to connect the dots so that that reading books and listening to CDs would prepare them to be equippers. I think I intuitively believed that if they filled their minds and hearts with a wealth of vision, insights, and skills, those ideas and ideals would spill out of them and affect those they worked with.

That's exactly what happened. Within a couple of weeks I began to see volunteers on their teams carrying around great books on leadership. I heard people in the halls saying, "Dude, you've got to hear this. Dan told me about this book he's reading, and it's awesome!" The excitement about developing people was in its infancy, but it was real. I watched enthusiasm grow organically and naturally as it overflowed from the hearts of my team.

When I describe what began to happen in our team during those first weeks, some people ask, "What had your team been doing? Hadn't they been developing leaders already?"

Not really. I had seen a few glimmers of leadership development by the people on our team, but as a whole, we stank. Don't get me wrong. We were completely committed to putting on great programs, having excellent services, visiting people in the hospital, and dozens of other ministries that staff members do. Those are *important* things, but they aren't the *essential* thing. We had neglected the one priority that would make everything else explode in vision and passion. I believe our first conversation finally put us on the right track.

The First Two Weeks

After our meeting, Dave had hung around until everybody left. I pulled some books off my shelf by authors I liked and told him what each one had taught me. Soon he had an armload of books and a heightened sense of anticipation of what he might learn from them. It was a hopeful start.

At our staff meeting a week after the first conversation, I told everyone how excited I was about where we were going as a team, and I affirmed their commitment to become multipliers. I told them again that I was sure God would use our plans to transform our team, the ministry teams they led, and the whole church culture. I realized that I needed to keep saying those things—in different ways at different times—to reinforce our new direction and establish a new culture.

Everyone seemed to be very excited as I handed out the list of twelve books I had picked for us to read as a team. A few staff members had read one or two of the books, and they looked at me as if to say, "Does that mean I have to pick another one?" I immediately assured them, "No problem. If you've already read one, just read it again so you'll be locked and loaded for our discussions each week."

I asked everyone to give me their lists of books and CDs. A few of them had completed their lists, but several were having trouble coming up with a list they could be excited about. "No sweat," I told them. "Keep working on it and bring it next week. Get some ideas from each other if you want to."

I knew that we needed to get off to a good start, so during those first two weeks I dropped by each person's office to ask, "Hey, what are you thinking about our goals? How do you feel about our direction?" Those were important conversations to show, first, that I really cared about each of my coworkers. I listened to their hearts, not just their words, and it helped me to gauge each person's level of buy-in. But the talks also helped everyone realize that I was going to birddog this strategy all day, every day. My presence and tenacity told them volumes about my commitment to them and where we were going as a team. Several of them let me know they got it.

Dave sat back in his chair and told me, "Scott, I'm fired up. I hadn't realized how many opportunities I have been missing with my team." He had inherited a leadership training meeting for youth volunteers I had started when I had his role at the church, so he was already a leg up on everybody else. He told me, "I've been coasting every week, but now I realize how important our training is. I see how I can do a much better job of equipping people and helping them to become multipliers. I'm excited. Let me at 'em!"

As much as anybody, Justin was moved by the vision. When I sat in his office, he immediately said, "Thanks, Scott. I've wanted to grow and become a better leader, but I didn't know how. Thank you for giving me a new vision for my life. I really appreciate your leadership. I want you to know that I won't let you down." He paused for a second as I nodded in gratitude for his affirmation. Then he asked, "I've been listening to great talks, but I haven't known how to put them into action. Will you help me?"

Isn't that the kind of question every pastor longs to hear? "You bet," I told him. "It's my pleasure. I believe in you. You have greatness in you, and I'm thrilled to help bring it out." I knew Justin had never felt that he quite fit in his role, so I said, "Justin, this process is going to develop your leadership abilities, and it will help you find your sweet spot in serving God." Our conversation that day reaffirmed my deep appreciation for his heart and my love for him. Even though he didn't feel confident, he was giving everything he had to please God. Who could ask for more?

When I popped into Joel's office to find out how he was responding to the first week on our new planet, he laughed and said, "This is a trip. I've never read so many books in my whole life!" I leaned in to hear what his follow-up statement was going to be, and he continued, "But hey, I'm all for it." His tone changed a bit as he promised, "Scott, I'll do the best I can. You can count on that." I sensed something of a flashing yellow warning light with his comment, but I chose to believe the best. "Great!" I answered. "That's what we're all doing—our very best."

The first change after our initial conversation—and probably the most important one—was that the people on my team were convinced I was committed to lead them in a new direction that would improve everything. This was especially true for Justin, Mark, and Dan. I could almost read their minds. I sensed no dread that they were being asked to do something hard. They loved it that I was asking them to dig deep and bring out their very best. They were thrilled that they finally had a leader who was taking them where they knew God wanted them to go. A few times when God has led me in a new direction, I've wondered, *Man, why didn't I think of this before?* That's how I felt when I saw my team's response during those first weeks. I knew we were doing exactly what God wanted us to do, and every person on the team (I thought) was 100 percent with me.

I'm not saying everybody had the same level of enthusiasm. In my world, wherever two or three are gathered in the name of Jesus, there are at least four to six different perspectives about anything we're trying to do. For instance, Richard was on board with the reading target because he already read about a hundred books a year. He read histories and novels in addition to books on spiritual life and leadership. Every night, he sat up until bedtime with a good book. No wonder he was excited about meeting our goal. He could probably get there in a couple of months. The task for Richard was to select books that were challenging. He bought most of his reading material at Half Price Books. He loved it when he could find a book for a quarter. Until we clarified the kinds of books we were going to read, his top criterion was price.

> In my world, wherever two or three are gathered in the name of Jesus, there are at least four to six different perspectives about anything we're trying to do.

Some of the people on our team, though, weren't readers. They were committed to reach the goal, not because it was easy, but because it promised to produce real change in their hearts and ministries. Their eyes were fixed on the future benefits, and they would slug through the difficulties of getting there.

Several of our guys were already listening to ten podcasts and CDs every week. They were hearing great teachers talk about important issues, but neither they nor I had seen significant benefits. They hadn't developed a hungry heart to capture the points and make them their own. Most of what they heard had registered as little more than entertainment. Now, with a much higher sense of calling and a purpose to become a multiplier, they listened with new ears and couldn't wait to put what they learned into action. Vision does that for people. We instinctively interpret high goals as a challenge or a threat.

When I walked into our staff meeting and presented a new vision to shift our team from workers to multipliers, they could have complained, "That's not fair! What you're asking me to do isn't in my job description. When you hired me, you didn't say a word about reading thirty-six books and listening to 104 messages. You don't have the right to demand that I do all this." If people have such an attitude, it takes a work of God to bring them around.

Truthfully, I had expected two guys on the team to react like that. When they didn't, I was initially surprised, and then I became a bit suspicious. My suspicions were well founded. One of them, I found out much later, was resistant to the core, but he nodded, smiled, and said, "You can count on me, Scott. I'm in!" The other was terrified he couldn't measure up, yet he wanted with all his heart to meet the challenge. He felt threatened, but he was determined to do whatever it took to meet the goals the team had set. All the rest were, I was convinced, completely with me.

The next week at our staff meeting, we talked about a couple of chapters from the first book on our list. They had read the chapters I had assigned, and we had an electric discussion! I don't know if we had ever had that level of interaction the whole time I had been at the church. Everybody, even Joel and Richard, participated at a high level. I left that meeting pumped up that we were going somewhere we had never been before.

Six Months After the Conversation

We continued to work through the books I had selected, wading through several chapters each week. At the end of each staff meeting, I assigned chapters for the next week so we stayed right on target. After six months we had covered six books and things seemed to be going well.

At about that time, though, I had a flash of fear. At first I had made an effort to "bird-dog" each person's progress, but I hadn't followed up lately. I had seen various staff members talking to people on their ministry teams about the things they were learning, so I assumed they were doing everything they had committed to do—but what if they weren't? What if we got to the end of the year and only one or two of them had fulfilled their commitment? Would I have the guts to fire most of my team? If I did, there might be a mutiny in our church, and I was pretty sure whose neck would be on the block!

Late at night for a week or so, I envisioned conversations with our board, with the staff members, and with their wives. I could imagine saying to our board, "Well, see, we all agreed to set this goal to improve our leadership abilities so the church would grow, and we set high standards of reading books and listening to messages to equip us. But this person and that one didn't do it, so I fired them."

Yeah, right. I felt like I was lighting a match in a dark gunpowder storage room. I imagined defending myself, "You don't understand. My motivation wasn't to threaten them so they would be fired. I only wanted to inspire them." That, I was convinced, wouldn't go over very well at all.

After some sleepless nights, I came in one morning and went straight to Justin's office. He looked at me as if to say, "Man, you look like you've been wrestling a bear all night, and you lost." But he tactfully waited for what I had to say. I asked, "Justin, how are you doing with all the books and CDs? Are they helping you? Are you on track with the numbers?"

He put his head down for a second, and then he slowly said, "Not really. I'm having a hard time. I honestly want to keep up, but I should be at eighteen and fifty-two right now, and I'm way below that."

"Bro," I told him with as much relief as anxiety, "come down to my office. I'll give you some books that will help you get back up to speed. And I'll help you any way I can." On the way down the hall, I asked, "Is anybody else struggling?"

Without missing a beat, Justin told me in a whisper, "I'm pretty sure Mark and Dave are both having a hard time, too."

I'm afraid I snapped a little. I barked, "You mean you guys have been talking to each other but not to me? You're having a hard time, and not one of you has said a word to me? Don't you know I'll do everything I can to help?" I paused for a second, and then I asked, "How's Brittany doing?"

Justin almost laughed, "Are you kidding?"

"Yeah, dumb question."

I motioned for Justin to follow me. When we got to my office, I told him, "Wait right here. I'll be back in a minute."

I went down to Mark's office, and I tried to be cool and calm as I asked, "Hey Mark, how's it going with your reading and messages?"

He took a deep breath, "Well . . . not as well as I'd like."

"Come down to my office," I told him. "I'll help you."

As he got up and started down the hall, I ducked into Dave's office. Again, I asked, "Hey, how's it going with your reading and CDs?"

He said, "Uh . . . pretty good."

"Pretty good?" The look on my face must have told him that I knew what was going on.

"Well . . . no . . . not really," he came clean. "Not very good at all if you want to know the truth."

I wanted to say, "Yeah, I'd like to know the truth, and I would have preferred to know it a few months ago!" Thank God, sometimes I don't say everything that's on my mind. All I said was, "Come down to my office. I'm helping Justin and Mark, and I'll be glad to help you, too."

When we got to my office, I had already said enough to chide them for not telling me they were having problems keeping up. I told them I was glad they were there, which was true, and I started pulling books off the shelf. While I was looking through all my books on leadership, I asked, "Okay guys, what do you need? Where are you on your goals?"

They were all well behind the pace needed to make the goals the team had set. I quickly tried to figure out which books fit each guy's life and role, and which books would be quick to read. Both criteria seemed equally important. I pulled down *Raving Fans* and *One Minute Manager* by Ken Blanchard and said, "These are outstanding books, and they won't take you long to read. They're perfect for you right now." I found about a dozen books, and passed them out. I told them, "When you're finished with yours, pass them along to the other guys."

Before they walked out with their stacks of books, I asked, "Hey, before you leave, let me ask: do you know anybody else who needs some help? I don't want to say anything in staff meeting if the others don't have a problem."

They all shook their heads. Justin spoke for the group, "No, I think we're the only ones."

I think that made him feel bad, but I wanted to end on a good note. I told them, "Guys, thanks for telling me what's going on. I want you to succeed more than anything in the world, but I can't help if you don't let me know what's going on." They nodded and went back to their offices. I had dodged another bullet.

Nine Months After the Conversation

Over the next several months I kept a more watchful eye on our team, attempting to detect if anybody seemed to be struggling. I checked with Justin, Dave, and Mark from time to time to see if they needed any more books, and they sometimes came to my office to get one or two. The team seemed to be doing pretty well, and I noticed that the level of "insight and passion overflow" was still strong. Almost every week I heard a random comment from someone in the church that one of the staff had shared a principle he had learned from a book or a message on CD. I was thrilled that the staff members weren't just going through the motions to check off the list and get it over with. They were soaking in the life-changing truths they were reading and hearing.

One day Richard came to my office with a question. "Scott, I've read about seventy-five books so far, but I'm having a heck of a time with the CDs. I don't even have a CD player, so I have to listen in my car. I'm way behind on the audio part of our goals. Can I read more books and listen to fewer CDs?"

I wanted to say, "Sure. No problem," but I realized it wasn't my call. I told him, "I don't have a problem with it, Richard, but you need to talk to the whole team about this. We made a commitment together, and any change needs to be made as a group."

I think he was a little perturbed that I didn't immediately give him the green light, but he responded, "Makes sense."

At the next staff meeting I announced, "Richard and I have been talking, and he would like to ask for a change in his goals for the year. Richard, tell them what you're thinking."

Richard told the group what he had told me, and we had a brief but lively discussion about the values of flexibility and commitment. In the end, the group agreed to let Richard read ninety books and listen to forty CDs. He was pleased, and the others felt lucky they didn't have to read ninety books!

The End of the Year

With one week to go in the year, I reminded our staff to bring their lists of books and messages to our next meeting. "Bring a copy for everybody," I told them. "I want everyone to see what you've read. You'll give each other some great ideas for the future." I reminded them that those who met the goal would get $500. We would also party for the rest of the day and go out for dinner that night. I looked around the room and saw confidence on their faces, so I was encouraged. "Dress casually," I said. "We're going to play golf or go bowling or do whatever you want to do."

The next week we all walked into the staff meeting with a sense of excitement—most of us, anyway. Since I never miss an opportunity to preach, I gave them a short pep talk about how proud I was of them and how I had seen each of them grow during the year. I let them know various people on their teams had told me of reading specific books recommended to them, and I drew a graph that showed our church had grown from 650 to 750 that year. We were on our way!

I said, "And now—drum roll, please—pass around your lists." As each person handed out his or her list to the group, I handed over a check for $500: Justin, Dave, Dan, Mark, and Brittany. Each person gave the others high fives. It was a great time!

Then it was Joel's turn. I held out one hand to take his list, and in the other I held his check. He only had one sheet in his hand. I thought, *Well, he probably didn't get around to making copies before the staff meeting. No big deal.* But that wasn't the problem. His piece of paper contained the titles of only a few books and messages, and he chuckled, "Yeah, I didn't get all of it done, but I'll tell you this: I read more books than I've ever read in my life, and I've listened to more CDs than ever, too. That's got to count for something."

I could see his list so I already knew the answer, but I asked so the whole group would know, "How many books did you read?"

"Twenty-two."

"And how many messages did you listen to?"

"Thirty."

"Okay. After we're done in a few minutes, I want to talk with you alone."

"Sure," Joel smiled with practiced nonchalance. "No problem."

The last person to report was Richard. Before I could ask him to give me his list, he stood up, raised his arms in victory, and bellowed, "Scott, bless God. I read ninety books this year!" It was his way of saying that he might not be as young as the rest of us and might not be as plugged into audio technology as the rest of us, but he had proven that he was as committed as we were. I kept from looking at the others in the room because we would probably have started laughing. "That's fantastic!" I told him with a straight face. A few others chimed in, "Man, Richard. That's awesome!" "Wow, that's incredible!" "Way to go, Richard. You are a reading maniac."

He wasn't quite as proud of his list of messages, so he just handed it to me. I looked at the list and told the group, "Forty-one CDs. Over the top, Richard. That's great!"

Justin then smiled and asked, "Hey Scott, what about your list? You *did* read some books and listen to CDs this year, didn't you?"

If I hadn't been so upset about Joel, I would have given him a sarcastic response, but my heart wasn't into humor at that moment. I said, "Yeah, I almost forgot. Here's my list." I picked up my lists from my desk and handed them out. I had read fifty-five books and listened to 170 messages. I couldn't think of any way to be funny so I simply said, "I really enjoyed a lot of those. If you want me to recommend some to you, I'll be glad to."

We were done. Everybody had given their reports and passed out their lists. Our celebratory mood, though, was tempered by tension in the room. I looked at everyone but Joel and said, "Way to go, guys. I'm so proud of you. Now, if you'll give Joel and me a few minutes, I'll meet you in the front."

As the six of them left, they ragged on each other the way teammates do when they just have won a big game. They looked at their checks and tried to grab them from each other. "The books you read were comic books," Mark kidded Justin.

"Yeah," Justin didn't miss a beat, "but at least mine had words in them. How many crayons did you use?" They had a good laugh, and it was great to hear them.

After the last one left the room, Joel and I were alone. I sat in a chair across from him, took a deep breath, and looked him in the eye. He started the conversation, "Well, hey, I did the best I could. You're not mad at me, are you?" He could tell I wasn't happy, so he continued, "Scott, I don't see why this is such big deal to you. I'm the director of media arts. My job isn't to develop leaders anyway."

I felt my neck getting a little warm. No matter how clearly and often I had stated our vision and goals all year, at that moment it became crystal clear he thought I had been bluffing. Everybody else got it, but Joel didn't.

I responded, "So you don't remember our discussions about all of us needing to develop leaders? You weren't listening when we talked—oh, about a dozen times this year—that this is a priority for all of us, even for you in media arts and Dave in the children's ministry?"

He knew better than to disagree, so he took a different tactic. He shook his head and said, "I don't see how reading books and listening to CDs has anything to do with leadership or my part of the church's ministry. It just doesn't make sense to me."

I wasn't going to let him off the hook with a lame excuse. "Joel, a year ago when I presented this vision and we talked long and hard about our plans, you said, 'Scott, count me in.' All during the year when we talked about doing whatever it took to reach our goals, you never voiced one word of concern or disagreement. As late as a few weeks ago, I asked everybody how they were doing and if they needed any help, and you said, 'No, I'm doing fine.'"

He had nothing to say because everything I was telling him was irrefutable truth. When I finished recounting the facts, I wanted to help him understand the damage he had caused. "Dude, what do I do with all this? You've failed the team. You broke covenant with each person who was sitting in this room a few minutes ago. How can we trust you after you lie to us continually for a year? How can we believe you when you tell us anything from now on?"

Joel glared at me. He probably hadn't had anybody talk to him like that in a long time, but I wasn't quite through. I pointed out the window. Mark had pulled around the church van and the group was loading up. "Do you see them?" I asked. "They're having a blast celebrating all they have done to reach their goals, but even more, they have seen what God has been doing in them and through them because they're filling their hearts with powerful leadership truths. Joel, our team is going somewhere. We're trusting God together for incredible things, but you don't seem to want to be a part of it."

By now he was aware that I hadn't been bluffing all year after all. He glared at me as I told him, "Joel, it's hard for me to hear you say, 'I don't get this emphasis on leadership development.' We have made it crystal clear that it is a core value of our team and our church. It determines where every ministry of our church is going, including yours. There's no way I can let you stay in such an influential position if you're not on board. In your role, you communicate the heart of our church to every person on Sunday morning and throughout our community. What you do really matters, and we need you to be completely devoted to our core values. Right now, you're not."

I was doing my best to speak the truth in love and follow the pattern of confrontation described in Matthew 18. With all my heart, I wanted to win my brother. My goal had never been to make anyone's life hard or find an excuse to fire someone. I wanted my coworkers to succeed more than they ever dreamed, and I had encouraged them to help shape the direction of our team's goals. So I wasn't going to mince words with Joel. If he had come to me during the year and asked for help, I would have moved heaven and earth to help him. But he hadn't asked for help, so I told him bluntly, "Brother, you lied to me and to the team. By not doing the work all the rest of us did, you've shown that you're either lazy or rebellious. I don't know which it is, but neither characteristic is good."

> My goal had never been to make anyone's life hard or find an excuse to fire someone. I wanted my coworkers to succeed more than they ever dreamed, and I had encouraged them to help shape the direction of our team's goals.

At that moment I had a flash of insight about Joel's ministry. Since he had joined our team a couple of years previously, I could recall numerous times when he had called on me, the senior pastor, to step in and take care of something in a pinch. He might need me to take some pictures, edit text for a brochure, or otherwise bail him out just before a big deadline. I had always been glad to help because I wanted to serve my team, but it wouldn't have been necessary if he had developed a strong team to work with him. Suddenly it dawned on me (I guess I'm a little slow) that his failure to follow through with the books and CDs was indicative of failure to do the necessary work in his ministry. I wondered if he had the same lackadaisical habits in his marriage and home life, but this conversation wasn't the time to bring it up. I figured problems might surface later—and they did, with a vengeance.

I reminded Joel of a number of times when he had called me to step in when he had no one else to help him, and I asked, "Do you see how all of this is connected? You haven't been developing people for your team, so your ministry has suffered. All the work our staff has agreed to do this year is to strengthen us so that we will have the heart, vision, and skill to build great teams in each ministry. Brother, you haven't been growing, and you've now shown that you aren't committed to grow."

I'd done quite enough talking, so I asked, "What do you want to say to me?"

He cocked his head and told me, with obvious anger, "Hey man, don't judge lest you be judged."

That really hacked me off, but I responded calmly, "Joel, you know that's not what Jesus was talking about in Matthew 7. Surely you have more to say to me than that."

He was still glaring, but he looked down, probably in disgust. "I don't know what to say. Nobody has ever talked to me this way." He looked back up and continued, "Scott, plenty of churches around the country want me, and I could go there today. I don't need you or this church."

I said calmly and slowly, "That may be true, but if you're going to stay on our staff team, you have to be sold out to the goal of developing people. And to do that, you have to be a great model of someone who loves God and is continually acquiring skills and principles to lead more effectively."

Joel and I had been more than members of the same team. Since the day he came, we had developed a friendship outside normal church activities. Our families loved each other. I think those ties had given him a sense of immunity from any threat that I was really serious. Now, he realized he had misread me.

It was time to end the conversation. I had said all the things I needed to say, except for describing the next steps for him. I pointed out the window, "Joel, do you see those people in the van? All of us drove ninety miles an hour toward our goals this year, and you went fifty. Today, you're behind. Next year, we're still going to go ninety miles an hour. Even if you go ninety, you'll still be behind. You're going to have to dig deep to catch up." I realized what I was saying. It was unrealistic to expect him to do twice as much as the rest of us the next year, so I told him, "If I see you working your tail off, that will tell me everything I need to know about your heart, and I'll be thrilled." I paused a moment to let this sink in, then I told him, "Think about it for a few days, and then let me know if you're in for next year."

I could tell he was angry because I didn't give him a pass. I had one more thing to say, and as I spoke, tears came to my eyes. "Joel, I'm so upset with you I don't know what to do. I love you like a brother, and you're breaking my heart. You're putting me in a very hard position:

You're making me have to choose between our friendship and the vision God has given us as a team. How dare you treat the people in the van and me like that? It has nothing to do with not being able to read or not having time to listen to CDs. It's all about your heart. We'll talk in a few days. I'm going to go have fun with the rest of the team. You can catch up on your reading. That would be a good way to spend your day."

I got up and left the room. My heart was heavy, but I was sure I had said what God wanted me to say. I had been strong, but not harsh. I had told Joel that I loved him—as if he didn't already know it from countless interactions over the past few years. But I hadn't let him off the hook. If I had, I would have betrayed the rest of the people on the team, my own calling as a leader, and my integrity before God.

In the sixty seconds it took me to walk down the hall and out the doors to get in the van, I had to make a monumental mental shift from correction to celebration. I didn't want my disappointment over Joel to taint my time with the rest of the team. When I jumped in the backseat of the van, I high-fived everybody and hollered, "We're going to have some fun today!"

I'm sure everybody wondered, *What happened to Joel? What did Scott say to him? And how did he respond? Is he still on the team?* But I didn't say a word about my talk with Joel. The spirit of that day was almost pure, unmitigated joy that we had done something magnificent together, and we were going where God was leading us. But beneath the smiles and kidding, we all felt a small, nagging sense of loss, of awkwardness, of doubt about how we would relate to Joel when we saw him next.

We went bowling, and all afternoon we laughed, talked, and ate stuff people should never put in their mouths. It was lots of fun. That night when we took our spouses out to a nice steak restaurant, I overheard a few of them ask, "Where's Joel?" But we didn't talk about it at all as a group.

At the end of dinner, I told our team, "You did a fantastic job this year, and God has blessed us. Each of us has already seen fruit in our own lives, our ministries, and in the growth of our church. I'm so proud of you I could pop! Next week we're going to talk about our goals and plans for the new year. I'll see you then. God has great things in store for us this year."

The First Year for Mark

Before the first conversation, it was as if members of our staff team operated in separate silos. We were working hard in our departments, and we coordinated our efforts when it was necessary, but we were a collection of individuals. The conversation suddenly brought us together as a team. We began working toward a common goal of becoming equippers and multipliers, and we wanted to support each other. I remember many discussions with people, especially Dan, when we told each other about particularly helpful books and inspiring talks. We became resources for each other. This, of course, led to some competition, but for the most part, I think it was healthy competition. We wanted to find the best resources and become the best leaders we could be. As the year went on, some of us wondered if a particular person or two would man up and complete the requirements. I hoped they would, but they didn't get involved in our conversations—or share our excitement—about the books and talks we found meaningful.

When I have told people about our goals for the first year, some have wondered how we picked the resources. It was fairly easy to pick the CDs because we had over a hundred excellent leadership talks in our church library. Finding the right books was more daunting. In the first week or two, some people asked Scott for recommendations. I just walked into his office and grabbed some books off his shelf. After a few weeks, though, most of us were eager to give quick book reviews to others on the team. We recommended most of the ones we read, but a few got thumbs down. This input prevented us from wasting time, focused our energies on productive, inspiring material, and built our relationships. (In the last few years, the pool of available resources in print, audio, and online has increased significantly.)

At some point during the year, I found a book called *The One Minute Millionaire* by Mark Hansen and Robert Allen. The authors combined clear principles with powerful stories about how to apply the concepts. The book, of course, focused on making wise financial decisions, but it was easy to apply the ideas to leadership development. The book helped me sharpen my perspective, set clear objectives, find a process to reach my goals, and make necessary adjustments along the way. One of the biggest lessons I learned from the book was the realization that I had lived under limited expectations. I had settled for **pretty good** instead of trusting God for **great** things. God could have used many different tools to teach me this lesson, but He had prepared my heart for the message of this book at that moment in my life.

Before that year, I had managed my time pretty easily, but the requirements our team had set forced me to be more diligent in planning my schedule each week. During the year, I never wondered if I was wasting my time with all that reading and listening. I have to admit that I had to think hard and plan well to carve out time to get it all in, but the payoff was well worth the effort.

Think about it . . .

1. What are some ways Scott kept his team on track during the first year?

2. What could he have done better to keep them motivated? How could he have anticipated their needs more effectively?

3. How would you have handled Richard's request for flexibility?

4. Did Scott's relationship with Joel cloud his perceptions during the year? Why or why not?

5. Do you feel comfortable with how Scott handled his conversation with Joel after the rest of the team left the room? What can you learn from this encounter? What would you have done and said if you had been Scott?

Chapter 3

Lessons Learned the First Year: The Carrot and the Stick

Overall, I was really happy with how our team had progressed that first year. I was hurt and angry with Joel, but I didn't want to let my disappointment with him overshadow the magnificent growth of the others. Brittany hadn't needed much encouragement to adopt the vision of becoming a multiplier; she was already doing it. I hoped our strategy would sharpen her skills and reinforce what she was doing with the women, and too, I hoped her heart and skills would rub off on the rest of the team. Several of our guys had made a monumental shift in the direction of their ministries, and to be honest, in the direction of their lives. They had a new sense of passion, and God had given them a clear path to improve their ministry strategy and skills.

As I reflect on the lessons I learned that year, my first impression was simply this: What took me so long? That's not a statement of discouragement, but of a profound sense of rightness. Sometimes I hear a speaker explain a point in the Scriptures or a ministry strategy and I think, *Man, why didn't I see that before? It makes perfect sense.* At those moments I know I'm in line with God's Spirit.

The first, and perhaps the most important, lesson from the first year was a profound sense of confidence that we were on the right track.

All year I had seen the new concepts change the way our staff led their teams. It's hard to read a book like *Good to Great* by Jim Collins or *Purple Cow* by Seth Godin and not have the concepts spill out of every pore of your body when you meet with people. I was thrilled every time I saw such a response. What follows in this chapter are some other important lessons I learned as I reviewed our first year.

A Clear Vision and a Challenging Strategy

I had been in countless staff meetings over the years when someone said, "We need to do a better job developing people." In the following weeks a few of the staff would make some efforts in that direction, but they soon reverted back to business as usual. For our team to see lasting change, I knew we needed more than that—much more.

We began by cleaning our glasses so we could take a long, hard look at reality—no excuses, no rationalizing. We had grown before, but we had always hit a ceiling. It was foolish and misleading to think (or tell our team) that we would grow if we "just worked a little harder." We needed a bigger vision and a better strategy, and the bedrock of our efforts had to be an honest appraisal of our history. We weren't growing past a certain point because we weren't the "horses" to take the church to the next level. Either our team would have to grow stronger and sharper, or we would have to find different horses to take us there.

The three classifications of church staff—workers, equippers, and multipliers—gave handles to the vision and propelled the strategy. Those terms created categories in our minds of what God has called us to be and do. The vision to become equippers, and eventually multipliers, created in our staff a hunger to learn. They didn't read books and listen to messages out of a sense of duty but because they desperately wanted to discover how to become better leaders so they could fulfill the vision God had given them.

As they read and listened, everything began to click. Their hearts were enflamed by the passion of the various writers and speakers they were now familiar with, and they couldn't help themselves—a renewed zeal for Christ and His cause overflowed from them. They led their teams differently. Their talks were deeper and more creative. Their personal interactions had more direction than ever before. They were becoming terrific models for everyone in their lives, including their families.

> The first stage of our strategy wasn't to sharpen skills but to fill our hearts. We couldn't pour out passion and insights we didn't possess.

My staff was now coming to me saying, "Scott, teach me how to do this and that." Their ministry team members were becoming just as hungry, asking *them* for help to become the people God wanted them to be. Thirst for God was becoming contagious. The first stage of our strategy wasn't to sharpen skills but to fill our hearts. We couldn't pour out passion and insights we didn't possess.

Clearly Define Each Element of the Vision, Strategy, and Plan

At our first conversation, I knew I would need to redefine certain terms for our staff. For example, the term *leadership* has become so common that many people don't understand what it means any more. I've heard people say that Shaquille O'Neal and Albert Einstein are examples of great leadership. One is a phenomenal athlete and the other one of the brightest geniuses of all time, but excellence in a field doesn't equate to leadership.

We spent time during those first weeks defining and discussing the differences between *workers*, *equippers*, and *multipliers*. Five of the seven staff members were workers at the beginning of that year, but if I had asked them, I'm sure they would all have claimed to be equippers, if not multipliers. Quickly for some, and gradually for others, the lights came on and they realized the need to make some drastic changes. Brittany was the exception. Most of the teambuilding the others started only affirmed what she was already doing. Still, she told me many times that she loved the direction we were going. I think she secretly wondered what took the rest of the team so long to get there, but she was much too kind to say it out loud.

During the year we talked often about three areas of leadership:

» *Spiritual life*—Walking with God, loving and serving Him with all one's heart instead of being driven by compulsion;

» *Strategy*—Understanding the goals of ministry and the process of reaching the vision God has given us; and,

» *Skills*—The nuts and bolts of the job for each person, whether managing the soundboard, teaching a small group, or doing crisis counseling.

All people need to grow in these three areas. We would begin with our staff, then their teams, and then succeeding generations of leaders in their ministries. We had talked about those areas many times before, but the rate of mental slippage had been significant. Now, with a new sense of God's calling and a strategy to build multiplying disciples, our staff listened more intently to every word they heard and retained what they learned.

Implement a Long-term Strategic Plan

Many staff teams plan for the next week or the next month. For most, a three-month plan is more than sufficient. But I knew that changing a culture wouldn't happen in a few months. I had a three-year plan in mind before we ever met that first time to talk about our vision, strategy, and goals. Implementing a plan over so much time would test our tenacity, but it would offer the only real hope for genuine change.

I knew we wouldn't see the kind of change God was calling us to make if I just talked briefly about vision during a few staff meetings. Our patterns had become firmly

> I had a three-year plan in mind before we ever met that first time to talk about our vision, strategy, and goals.

entrenched, and changing them required massive effort. We spent time defining a clear vision: growing the church to 1,000 people. We articulated the strategy: moving from workers to equippers to multipliers. And as a team, we created a plan for the first year to fill our hearts and minds with truth from thirty-six books and 104 messages so we could become excellent models for the people we lead. By connecting the vision, the strategy, and the goals, our leaders understood why they were reading and listening. It wasn't just to check off boxes. It was to prepare them to become great models for the people on their teams, and eventually, to multiply their effectiveness through several generations of leaders.

I chose the 1,000-person target for church growth because it was one we had never achieved before, yet the number wasn't so high that it was ridiculous. We had hit 900 several times, but we hadn't sustained or grown beyond that level. Setting the bar at a consistent attendance of 1,000 challenged us to lead better and forced us to depend on God—not a bad combination. Goals need to be both challenging and attainable. If they're too easy to reach, they don't demand a team's creativity and best efforts; if they're too hard, they discourage people instead of inspiring them.

Some people might think the 1,000-person goal was just an arbitrary number. It was in a sense, yet it fit our church and our situation. We didn't set a crazy goal of growing to 20,000, and we didn't require the growth to 1,000 within a certain period of time. I believed that we kept hitting a barrier for one reason: we weren't building enough competent leaders to take us past 650. I also believed God wanted us to make an impact on our community. The kingdom of God and the salvation of people was our ultimate concern, not raw numbers. The numerical goal just gave us a benchmark to shoot for.

> I was convinced, as I said dozens of times in many different ways, that if we developed a growing contingent of passionate, skilled leaders, we would become the church God wanted us to be.

I was convinced, as I said dozens of times in many different ways, that if we developed a growing contingent of passionate, skilled leaders, we would become the church God wanted us to be. We would reach our community. We would send people to reach the world for Christ. The number only gave us a way to measure our growth. I was sure we would grow far beyond 1,000. Indeed we have, because our staff became multipliers that expanded the kingdom of God. Everything else was a means to that end.

Be Prepared

I spent months formulating my approach for the first conversation. I believe God orchestrated the concepts I shared that morning from the raw material of dozens of books, CDs, conferences, and countless conversations with friends and mentors who shaped the direction of my thinking. It wasn't the result of a single book I had read or a sudden flash of thought. When I met with our team the morning of the first conversation, I was convinced, in the core of my being, that God had given me a conviction that things needed to change, insight about the role of our staff in building leaders, and a strategy to take us where He wanted us to go. Those months of preparation gave me confidence that God was right in the center of this plan.

As I looked in the Scriptures, I thought immediately of 2 Timothy and Ephesians 4. As I read and prayed, the Lord reminded me of the account of Jethro telling Moses to select competent men to help lead the people (Ex. 18). When Moses died, he left Joshua to lead the Israelites in the conquest of the Promised Land. But when Joshua died, he left Israel with a leadership void. No wonder Scripture says, "The people did what was right in their own eyes," and the nation suffered. The historical accounts of God's people illustrate the principle of equipping and multiplying. Some leaders did a great job of raising up a generation of leaders, but many failed miserably. David's "mighty men" and his preparation of Solomon show that he was a competent leader. In contrast, the series of kings who came later were mostly unprepared and uninterested in spiritual things, which became obvious in their weak and ineffective leadership.

Jesus, of course, poured His life into a handful of men, and those few changed the world. His last words commanded them to make disciples who would take the gospel to everyone on the planet. Paul, perhaps the toughest hombre the church has ever known, had a tender heart. Everywhere he went, he found leaders and equipped them to multiply. His method wasn't academic. He poured out his heart to them, and he modeled the life God wanted them to live. He wrote the Thessalonians something they already knew from watching him: "We were gentle among you, like a mother caring for her little children. We loved you so much that we were delighted to share with you not only the gospel of God but our lives as well, because you had become so dear to us" (1 Thess. 2:7–8).

> Each of us has only a finite amount of time, and God will hold us accountable for how we use it.

Part of a leader's preparation includes walking into the first conversation with a powerful biblical mandate for developing leaders. That morning I only used two passages, but as the year progressed, we talked about many others to strengthen our grip on God's calling.

Each of us has only a finite amount of time, and God will hold us accountable for how we use it. We don't have the luxury of wasting it on people who don't want to grow, equip others, and multiply their leadership to several generations. Throughout the history of God's people, He has used men and women to change the world. He isn't asking us for anything less today.

Use Word Pictures

I love to hear people tell stories, and I benefit from a well-crafted metaphor when someone is trying to communicate a point. As I prepared for the first conversation, God gave me some word pictures: the bucket representing our church with holes in it at 650, the basketball goal set at ten feet, and my responsibility of building stairs so everyone on the team could dunk the ball. These metaphors certainly helped me as I thought about the best way to share what I wanted to say, and I'm sure it helped them (even Brittany, who doesn't care much about basketball) understand where we were going and how we would get there.

Some members of a staff team may be auditory learners, but most people benefit from visual images. It's helpful to use a whiteboard to draw pictures, write goals, and make lists. You may have to erase the board several times during a long staff meeting, but leave the most important components that are the centerpiece of the new vision, strategy, and goals. I drew the bucket with the holes, the basketball goal, and the steps to reach the basket. During the talk that day, I wrote and erased other things on the rest of the board as we kept talking about our strategy. Keeping those images on the board, though, kept our vision clear and strong throughout the discussion.

Involve the Team in Determining the Goals

As I laid out the vision for our future, I could have just told my staff members how many books to read and messages to listen to, but that would have been a big mistake. For them to own the goals, they had to shape them. I told them what I do, and I let them talk about what they wanted to do. If they had suggested goals that were too big, I would have stepped in to help them back down a bit. And if their goals were too low, we would have had a frank discussion about the nature of commitment. Thankfully, I didn't have to correct their goals—then or later. To be honest, I wasn't sure what their goals should be, but at the end of the discussion, they were in the ballpark of what I thought was good and right for them. The number wasn't as important as the sense that they were committed to being stretched. The goals they determined were thirty-six books and 104 messages. If they had come up with twenty-five books and eighty messages, I would have been fine with that. But if they had said twelve and twenty, I would have questioned their commitment to excellence, and we would have talked about how much we needed to soak up before we could pour enough out for others.

When I asked them to talk about the goals they wanted to set, I listened for their input. I wanted to assess their perceptions and motivations. I asked every person for his or her suggestion about the number of books and CDs. As they spoke, I could tell if they were excited about the direction we were going, or if they were resistant. Another benefit of letting them talk with minimal input from me was that the goals they set were theirs, not mine. I wasn't coercing them or controlling them. After they determined what to do, I became their cheerleader and resource to help them reach the goals *they* had set.

Provide a Carrot and a Stick

Promised rewards and somber warnings are both important, but be sure to scream loudly and often about the carrot, and minimize your emphasis on the stick. Don't get them reversed. People need to know that you want them to succeed and that you'll do everything possible to help them reach their goals. Come up with a reward that's meaningful to them. As I thought and prayed about it before we met, it seemed good to me to offer a check for $500 and a day of celebration. If that works for you and your team, go for it. If not, come up with something else.

> People need to know that you want them to succeed and that you'll do everything possible to help them reach their goals.

Some pastors might think, *Whoa, that's a lot of money for each staff member!* Not really. If the productivity of a staff member goes up by 50 percent over two or three years, that is a terrific return on a $500 investment. Besides, some of the people on our team spent about that much on books and CDs during the year, so the check only reimbursed them for their expenses. Paying them back was the least we could do.

When I explained the "stick" of the first conversation to a pastor, he said, "Threatening them with firing? Isn't that kind of harsh?" It certainly would be, but that's not what I did. I told them, "If you don't meet your goal, I'll give you ten minutes to tell me why I should keep you on staff." And that's exactly what I did with Joel.

The kingdom is serious business. People's eternal destinies are at stake. Like everyone else, I want people to like me, but I'm well aware that some day I will answer to God. On that day, only one evaluation will matter—not my staff team's, my board's, my wife's, or my own. On that day, I want to hear Jesus say to me, "Well done, Scott! You've been a faithful servant. Enter into the joy of your Master."

The Scriptures are full of carrots and sticks—incredible blessings for those who choose to honor God, and significant consequences (now and later) for those who are lazy or rebellious. I always have to check my heart to be sure I'm not delighting in "lording it over" my staff. That's sin—no need to rationalize it. But if I'm going to be the leader God wants me to be, my communication with my staff will mirror the motivations outlined in the New Testament. Strong leadership may sometimes arouse suspicions, but weak leadership should, too. The demand to control is just as bad as a paralyzing fear of failure. In either case, the leader needs to repent.

Provide a Resource List

One thing I wish I had done better is to help my staff members find books and CDs that thrilled them. I read tons of books. I love some of them, but a few are dogs. I was able to help Dave find some books on that first day that gave him a sense of direction and excitement. I wish I had done that for everybody.

The team designed the goals, and we could have helped each other more. When we met the week after we set our goals, I should have asked everyone to bring a list of their favorite books, CDs, podcasts, and videos to help the rest of the team come up with great lists of their own. I guess I didn't do that because I have hundreds in my own library, and I simply didn't think they needed help coming up with a great list. I was wrong. It wouldn't have taken more than a few minutes to pass lists around and highlight a few from each person. I'm afraid that some of the struggles Justin, Dave, and Mark had during the year were the result of not having confidence that the books and CDs on their lists were worth the trouble of reading and listening to.

Be Firm and Direct but Flexible When Necessary

I have no idea how I would have responded if I had been forced to make a decision when Richard asked if he could read more books and listen to fewer CDs, but I didn't have to make that choice. The team had come up with the goals, so I referred his request to them. It's interesting, though, that none of the others ever pushed back on the goals for the year. They obviously felt that they all had input, and the team had made a decision together. I offered my input as well, but they were firm in their plans. I was proud of their willingness to listen carefully to Richard's request. They asked him for his suggestion for the change. It seemed reasonable, so they accepted it. That moment was another step forward for our team. They all (or almost all) owned the vision individually and corporately. With a foundation of confidence, they listened well and allowed a reasonable change for one person on the team.

Don't Underestimate the Impact of Spouses

Some staff members never take their work home with them. They don't tell their spouses what's going on with the team, they don't talk about conflicts, and they don't share their frustrations. There are possibly two or three such people across the country, but not many. Most go home and spill their guts. They want to feel supported and understood, and they understandably enlist their spouses as allies.

I certainly should have been more aware that Joel had told his wife about our vision and goals—but only from his slanted perspective. It didn't cross my mind to meet with him and his wife, Kim, to talk about the future after he failed to live up to his commitment. It would prove to be a costly mistake, but I was still unaware of the storm that was brewing—a storm that would break as a human resources "hurricane" a year later.

If I had it to do over again, I would have invited the entire team and their spouses to a dinner at the beginning of the year to share my heart with all of them and answer any questions. Sometimes spouses ask much more pointed questions than team members, and that's perfectly fine with me. I would much rather deal with hard questions and speak to people's concerns than let assumptions fester into misunderstandings and resentments. It's wise to nip negative presumptions in the bud.

Ever since I saw the importance of informing spouses about a new vision for the church and our team, I have also begun including them when I feel there is any risk of misunderstanding. The staff member, the spouse, and I meet for coffee and casual conversation. I explain to the spouse that I value his or her influence and perspective. I share my heart, and I answer any questions. This has proven to be a valuable way to smooth over misconceptions and avoid the potential for hurt feelings, and it has set a precedent that spouses can talk to me about anything on their minds.

The principle is this: If you have any inclination that a staff member might provide a biased version of the team's conversation to his or her spouse, take action to invite the spouse and staff member in for a chat. As I look back, I see there were several yellow flags in Joel's statements and attitude throughout the year, but I chose to "believe the best" instead of being shrewd.

Don't Overlook Signs of Resistance or Struggle

Speaking of yellow flags, I'm a visionary and an optimist. I believe most people have great hearts and will do what they commit to do. Such trust in others may sound noble and good, but the downside is that I often miss subtle (and not-so-subtle) comments and body language that would alert a more perceptive leader that the team member isn't really on board. You may call me naïve or foolish. Either way, the fact is that I overlooked several signs I shouldn't have missed.

Joel had been pretty quiet during the first conversation, and when he spoke he didn't seem threatened by the challenge of the new direction. I can see now that he was letting everybody else speak up while he disengaged. At the end of the conversation when I asked for commitments, he said the right things, but his intonation and body language showed resistance. I should have noticed. While I might not have said anything in that setting, I certainly should have called him in after the meeting to voice my concerns.

I asked him several times during the year how his reading and listening was coming along, and each time he cocked his head a little and said, "No problem." I interpreted his actions and words as confidence, almost nonchalance, but he was actually blowing me off. If I had properly read the tea leaves (and more important signals), I would have asked, "Would you show me the list of books and CDs you've read so far? I would like to see which ones appeal to you." I could have done dozens of things to address Joel's resistance earlier if I hadn't taken his words at face value.

But even more importantly, I had been missing signs during the previous two years we had worked together. In all that time I never saw a passion for excellence in his job in media arts, and he certainly hadn't expressed a commitment to develop leaders. He tried to get by, doing the least he could do. Why would I think all this would change because I gave an impassioned speech to the team? When he said he was on board, I at least should have assumed that this was a major shift from his usual passive performance. If I had thought he was making a cataclysmic change of attitude and leadership style, I should have offered much more individualized help. But I missed it all.

I should also have anticipated the difficulties some of the other staff members might experience in following through with their commitments—not because they were rebellious or lazy, but because they lacked confidence and had not yet developed the habit of feeding their minds and hearts. It took me six months to realize three of them were struggling. That was far too long. I should have been more aware of their frustrations so I could have helped them sooner.

Earn the Right to Change Directions

Pastors who are new to a church shouldn't try to change the direction of the church until they first build relationships and earn the trust of the staff. Some might argue, "It's better to come in with your guns blazing," but I think that's a mistake. All godly and effective leadership is based on respect and relationship. You can move mountains with a mutually supportive team; otherwise, you're always looking over your shoulder to see if anybody is following, or worse, who's trying to get you. When people see you as a person of integrity, they feel safe asking questions, and they follow more eagerly. But if they have reason to question your integrity, they wonder about your motives and resist your efforts to implement change.

> When people see you as a person of integrity, they feel safe asking questions, and they follow more eagerly.

New pastors should take a year to listen, model, and create a foundation to build on. During that year, they should ask the staff for an assessment of the strengths and needs of the church and their areas of ministry. Some will be very perceptive, a few will be brutally honest, but others will say only what they think the leader wants to hear. Maybe in subsequent conversations, pastors can establish guidelines for evaluations: honesty and hope, but no grumbling Eeyores and no "happy talk."

The assessment of the staff then becomes raw data for a "State of the Church" talk at the beginning of the first conversation. You can say, "Jim, you told me that . . ." "William, you observed . . ." "And Suzanne, you said you had seen . . ." Staff members will feel valued, even as you shake up their world with a fresh vision for the future. To embrace the change, they have to agree with the assessment that things aren't what God intends them to be. A sense of holy discontent is essential if your staff team is to long for change instead of resisting it.

The first year needs to focus on soaking in truth and passion so it can overflow from each staff member to their ministry teams. The pastor, though, has to model it first. If he walks into the first conversation and says, "Hey, it's all new to me too, but we're in it together," the strategy will not work. For at least a year or so, pastors need to meet those goals in their own lives. Then as they tell the staff what they are learning and how excited they are to implement the truths they have read and heard, the others will be ready to go when asked to set goals to fulfill a God-given vision for the church.

Realize that many people naturally resist change. Staff members may not say so, but during the first conversation many of them are thinking, *Hey, this isn't what I signed up for. It's not in my job description. What's the deal?* We have to earn the right to create a new deal they will understand and embrace.

Set the Bar High for New Hires

It's a principle of human resources that people instinctively internalize the standards and customs that are present on their first day in a new job. If the bar is high, they live according to high expectations the whole time they work in that environment. But if the bar is low when they begin, they will presume that is normal.

Pastors who plant churches have the privilege of establishing norms for their teams from the beginning. Of course, they have to deal with some steep challenges that pastors of established churches never face, but they can at least choose whom they want to serve on their staff and create the culture from Day One.

Pastors who hire new staff for existing staff teams need to be sure they don't create a disparity of expectations between the old staff and the new hires. You're surely in for problems if you give new staff hires high expectations and a clear, compelling vision when the rest of the team isn't on board with the new vision. So create the culture of leadership development you want before you hire anyone new. Then you'll all be on the same page together.

Get the Board Involved

I wanted to shift the focus of our board from overseeing the details of church business to assuming the role of spiritual shepherds of our flock. They were thrilled when I told them about our staff's vision, strategy, and goals. When I added, "And I want to do the same things with you," they looked shocked. But then I said, "It's all about feeding your minds and hearts so you overflow the love and power of God into the lives of the people around you each day. I'd like us to read and discuss twelve books this year." They were relieved that I wasn't expecting them to do as much as our staff, but they were also excited when they realized we were all on the same team, heading in the same direction, and with the same calling to become multipliers.

I blew one aspect of my relationship with the board that year. After I had to have the hard conversation with Joel, I didn't tell any of them about it. I left them in the dark. It was a mistake that would later come back to bite me.

Never Apologize for Aiming High

When Paul went to a city, he had a clear strategy: preach the gospel to anyone who would listen, raise up leaders to take over the church after he left, and care for every person—widows and orphans, the weak and the strong. He never apologized for asking leaders to be all they could be for the glory of God.

It's not enough to train workers, or even to build people into equippers. We need to find people who have the heart and skills to build strong leaders who will produce leaders of leaders of leaders. That's the way the world has been reached so far, and it's not going to change anytime soon.

A friend of mine created what he calls "The Negative One Differential Factor of Leadership" based on his observation that we are attracted to people who are farther along than we are in a given area. Because we are all continually growing, leaders don't attract and build people who rate higher than they do. So in terms of leadership, if I'm a seven on a scale of ten, I'll seek out someone who is an eight. And I'll be able to mentor someone who is a six or below.

> We need to find people who have the heart and skills to build strong leaders who will produce leaders of leaders of leaders.

I want people on my staff team who are at least an eight on a leadership scale of one to ten. Such leaders have the capacity to attract and build sevens, who can then work well with people who are sixes. If no one on my team rates higher than five, we're destined to have only ones, twos, threes, and fours as volunteers on all of our ministry teams. That's the way leadership works. We're attracted to those we admire; we attract those who are much like us—only one notch lower in leadership passion, skills, and capacity.

When we had our first conversation, most of our staff members weren't eights yet. It was my job to help them reach their highest potential—not only for their own sakes, but as they multiplied, for the sake of generations of leaders under them. It took a while for some of them to get there, but by the end of three years most of them had taken incredible strides.

These were important lessons during the first year. Some applied to my preparation prior to the first conversation, a few applied to the conversation itself, and many applied to the implementation of the plan during the year. All of these lessons, though, shaped the direction of our team and created an environment of excitement so that we could make real progress. As we ate together the night they turned in their lists, I could tell they were excited! There was something categorically different about our team. They were proud, in the best sense of the word, to be part of something exciting, something that challenged their socks off, and something that promised to make a huge impact for the kingdom. I could tell they loved being part of a team that was giving all we had to Christ. For me, it was one of the most heartwarming and thrilling days of my life—and I knew we were only getting started.

The one thing I wished I had done better was talk to each person every month—or at least once each quarter—to see how he or she was progressing in reaching our goals. Every month at a staff meeting I could have gone around the room and asked people to tell about a book or CD that had been particularly meaningful to them. It would have been very easy to do, but I didn't do it. When I finally talked to them, several had been struggling for months. By the end of the year, however, some great things had happened. We were ready for the second conversation—most of us, at least.

Mark Looks Back on the First Year

It took a year of diligent reading, listening, and reflection, but at the end of the first year I realized I had been no more than a worker. I had been the center of my efforts—if I didn't do something, it didn't get done. The first ray of light came in the initial conversation, but at that point I didn't want to admit I wasn't an equipper. As the months went by, the light became clearer, and my actions showed that I was doing most of the ministry work on my own. However, by the end of the year, I was realizing what it meant to be an equipper. The transformation had begun, but it couldn't have started without an honest (and painful) appraisal that I had been only a worker.

Most of the books I read that year were about business leadership, and most of the messages were spiritual and inspirational. I learned a lot from all of them. Truth is truth, and it was easy to bring the secular principles of leadership into the church setting and use them to honor Christ and build His people.

I have to say that I don't think I would have learned and grown as much if Scott hadn't challenged us to reach for more. He motivated us to grow as Christians and leaders, but I would have settled for less. The push of reaching our goals and the encouragement of our team were instrumental in my growth that year.

I would encourage pastors who are thinking about using this training model to carefully tailor it to fit their church and their staff teams. The principles are more important than the form. In the first conversation, Scott gave us an accurate analysis of our church's pattern of growth (or lack of growth). He introduced the clear and powerful concept of moving from workers to equippers to multipliers. Instead of demanding, "Hey, start being multipliers," he inaugurated a long-term process to saturate our minds and hearts in truth. Then, as we internalized the concepts, we were ready, willing, and finally able to take the next step to become equippers. Too often, leaders try to force institutional change by fiat, but organic growth doesn't happen that way. It requires new patterns of thinking, a negotiated buy-in, new ways of leading, a model to show how it's done, and plenty of time to process it all. Scott gave us all that.

The metaphor of dunking a basketball was really powerful for me. It would have been deflating if Scott had just said, "You need to dunk the ball. Come on. You can do it!" I knew I couldn't, no matter how hard I tried. He was brutally honest about the failure of our team to lead more people, but he didn't stoop to blaming or cheerleading. He gave us a process—a three-year process—to go from vision to reality. Finally, we had a realistic appraisal of our current condition and a hope-filled plan to achieve something special. It was a new day for Scott's leadership, our team, and our church.

Think about it . . .

1. How would you describe Scott's preparation in the weeks and months leading up to the first conversation?

2. What are the lessons he learned about setting a clear vision for numeric growth, the strategy of building multipliers, and the plan of reading and listening to fill their hearts with leadership principles?

3. How would you handle having a team set their goals for reading and listening to messages?

4. What are the most important lessons Scott implemented?

5. Are there any you disagree with or think are irrelevant?

6. Why is it crucial to earn respect and build strong relationships before you have the first conversation?

7. Now that you've read the chapters on the first conversation, the story of the first year, and the lessons learned, write out your implementation plan for the first conversation.

Chapter 4

The Second Conversation: Get Set

Our staff was returning to the church after celebrating the progress of the first year of our new leadership strategy. I told them again while they were together in the van, "I'm so proud of all of you. I asked you for a lot, and you brought your best. That's fantastic! In next week's staff meeting, we're going to talk about our plans for this year."

They were excited about the past year, and naturally they were curious about what was coming. Brittany smiled and spoke for all of them, "You can't leave it at that, Scott. Come on, tell us what's up."

I laughed, "No way."

They all got on my case, asking for a hint at what our plans would be. But I didn't bite. I wanted to sustain the mystery about their future. "Just show up next week. Don't worry; it'll be great."

When they saw they weren't going to get anything else out of me, they stopped asking for more. Prior to our meeting the following week there was an air of excitement on the team. They stopped me in the hall or came by my office with encouraging comments:

» "Man, this past year has changed my life."

» "Thank you so much for pushing me. I can see tremendous results already, and I can't wait to see what's going to happen next."

» "This is so cool. My wife told me I'm not the same person I was a year ago. Thanks so much."

» "My ministry team is as excited about the coming year as I am. They appreciate the fact that I'm building them as leaders instead of dumping stuff I don't want to do on them. It's made a difference— in me, in them, and in us. I can't wait to see what we're going to do this year. Let's get it on!"

» "Next year, let's read fifty books and listen to 150 messages!"

It was all I could do to keep my mouth shut and not reveal my plans for the coming year.

When they walked into my office for our staff meeting, I had the whiteboard cleaned and ready. As they approached, I overheard them talking about their goals for this year. They assumed we would have a similar plan, except with more books and CDs. But I had other ideas.

By Way of Review

Everybody except Joel had a facial expression like someone getting ready to play in a championship game. They were sober, yet pumped up because they knew the stakes were high.

I began by saying, "Okay, let's review where we started and how far we've come." I wrote "1,000" on the board beside a bucket with holes on the side. I told them, "We began to make changes because we saw that we were stuck at 650 people. No matter how hard we worked and what great programs we used, we always leaked down to 650. That was the capacity for our staff team. We agreed we weren't going to grow beyond that unless we changed, unless we became equippers and multipliers instead of workers."

I wrote those three words on the board and continued, "But the first step to becoming equippers and multipliers is becoming people worth following. We had to become great models to our people. That was our primary focus all last year—soaking in truth, grace, and leadership principles until we were so full that they spilled out of us to everyone we met." They were nodding. I explained that we had already grown to 750, and it was because their people were becoming outstanding leaders. Our capacity was already increasing. They were making a difference in their ministry teams' lives!

My speech was no longer news to them. By now they had heard it a dozen times or more, but they were excited to hear it again. I hope they felt it was like hearing a beloved grandfather tell stories over and over about his childhood—except that I'm not that old.

To be honest, I had been afraid there would be tension in the room because Joel hadn't done what the others had done. From time to time I looked over to see how he was responding. In the past, he almost always made jokes and kidded people when we got together, but in this meeting he was as silent as a tomb. The rest of the team didn't try to cheer him up or plead with him to get his act in gear. It seemed obvious their attitude was, "We're going for it. If you want to come, that's cool. But if not, we're not slowing down. It's entirely up to you." They weren't going to let Joel be an anchor holding the team back. I was thrilled (and relieved) by their attitudes.

I drew a basketball goal on the board and told them, "None of us can dunk, but we're not lowering the goal to make it convenient for us. We're keeping the goal high, but we've started building steps to help us get to the goal." They were nodding, but they couldn't wait for me to turn the corner from history to the future. Now was the time.

Figure 5

Plans for This Year

I asked, "What do you think our plans should be this year?" I sat down so they would know I wasn't looking for quick answers.

They had their responses ready. Various people spoke, but their answers were very similar: "We did thirty-six and 104 last year. This year we'll read fifty books—at least forty-five—and listen to 150 messages. After the growth we saw last year, imagine what we'll see if we do even more!"

I told them, "Wow, I'm so encouraged that you want to grow! And I'm thrilled that you're so committed to do whatever it takes to fill your hearts and minds with great stuff. We're going to keep it up, but we also have additional priorities this year." I went to the whiteboard and pointed to the three words: *workers, equippers, multipliers.* I crossed out "workers," and next to it, I wrote "model" **(figure 5)** I told them, "Right now, you aren't workers any more." There were a couple of exceptions in the room, but I chose to address the ones who had proven faithful. "You are models for your teams. This year we're going to focus on taking the next step: equipping your teams so they can become as effective as possible in their ministries."

They were really excited now. They were moving out of Triple A ball and headed to the Major Leagues, but I wanted to make sure they understood the bigger picture. I explained, "Don't miss this. I'm not saying we're going to stop with equipping. That's not our ultimate goal."

I heard a couple of them say the word *multiplier*, and I told them, "That's exactly right. If we're going to become multipliers, who are the people we need to select to equip?"

Their eyes got instantly wider. They got it. Justin said, "People who have the capacity to lead and equip others."

Brittany said simply, "Second Timothy 2:2."

"Exactly!" I was so delighted with them I almost popped. "If we're going to become multipliers, wise selection is essential. We need to pour ourselves into people who already have the capacity to multiply, or who can develop that capacity. What I'm doing with you is what you need to do with your people." We all took a few seconds for a deep breath as we pondered the new level of our strategy.

I asked, "How many of you gave a book or a CD to somebody last year because it touched your heart or gave you an insight about leadership?" They all nodded or raised a hand, so I continued, "I know you did. I saw people with books and CDs you gave them, and I heard them talk about how much your example inspired them. You already have a head start on this year's goal: equipping people to be more and do more for God's glory. It's so cool!"

They were already thinking of their teams and what they wanted to do to equip them. We were ready to dive into the specifics.

Who, When, and How

I went back to the board and pointed to the three levels of leadership. I said, "Just as you will find workers, equippers, and multipliers on church staffs, you will also find them on ministry teams. I told you a year ago that by now we would no longer have any 'workers' on *our* team. Now I'm saying that's *your* goal for the coming year: A year from now, you shouldn't have any 'workers' on your ministry teams. They should all at least be 'equippers.'"

I asked Mark to turn to Ephesians 4:11–13 and read the passage I had read to the group a year earlier. He read: "It was he who gave some to be apostles, some to be prophets, some to be evangelists, and some to be pastors and teachers, to prepare God's people for works of service, so that the body of Christ may be built up until we all reach unity in the faith and in the knowledge of the Son of God and become mature, attaining to the whole measure of the fullness of Christ." When he finished, I explained, "That's your goal, your priority, and your calling for this year."

Justin asked the poignant but obvious question: "How do we know we have the right people on our teams right now?"

"Great question," I said. And it leads us to today's focus. I want us to talk about three factors that shape the equipping of others: *who*, *when*, and *how*. You started at the right place, Justin. Let's talk about *who* we have to 'build up.' Any ideas?"

We began a lively conversation about how to tell if we had chosen our team members wisely. Some could point right away to the few blue chip players on their teams whom we all knew were already equipping volunteers. But it gradually dawned on almost everybody that they had people who had shown no promise of leadership. They were willing volunteers who arrived on time with a smile and were ready to set up chairs, give out handouts, work the sound system, and pitch in as needed ... but they hadn't shown an ounce of leadership capacity. Justin observed, "Well, to be honest, it's not necessarily their fault. Maybe I haven't given them the tools and vision they need to be leaders. Right now, it's on me."

I jumped in. "This year I want each of you to identify five key team members who already have proven to have a capacity to multiply by equipping others. Or you can focus on those in whom you are willing to invest extra time and energy to help become equippers and multipliers."

After I let that sink in a moment, I tried to help them think more specifically. "Dan, you have three student ministry interns. Those, I assume, are three of your five." He nodded. "So you need to determine which two other volunteers you want to be part of your five."

Dan said, "I'd probably like to have more than five. Seven probably."

"Okay. But don't dilute yourself too much. Equipping is more about

> Equipping is more about quality than quantity.

quality than quantity. It's much better to work with a few who really get it than a bunch who only get it halfway."

"I understand," he said thoughtfully. I could tell the wheels were turning.

"And Brittany, what are you thinking about this plan? You already have a team of leaders who lead other leaders."

She replied immediately, "But I can do a better job of equipping the people we have now. And one or two may be in over their heads. I need to think, pray, and talk to our leadership team about selecting the right women. This will be very helpful to us."

I moved on. "Dave, you have four people who are key leaders: those in charge of the nursery, administration, grades K through 3, and grades 4 through 6."

He jumped in, "And my assistant. That's five. That's my team."

"Cool. You're ready to go."

Next was our worship leader, Mark. I asked, "Mark, how does this apply to you?"

"Right now, we have one band of dedicated musicians. I appreciate all the time and effort they put in, but I need to develop other bands so we can rotate and take the load off that one group."

"And sound and lights?"

"Yeah, I need to put together teams that work well together, who enjoy what they do, and who do it for the Lord."

"Terrific."

Justin volunteered, "I have a team of seven people right now. We made some progress this past year just because I told them stuff I was learning. But I've been pretty happy with any warm bodies up to now. I sure haven't made it a priority to be intentional about selecting and equipping my team."

"So you need to do some thinking and praying about the composition of your team."

"Yeah," he was thinking hard now. "We might need to make some changes."

I turned to Richard. "You have a team of Sunday school teachers."

I could tell he had been thinking hard about how all this related to him. "Well, it's not really a team. We don't meet together that often."

"But each of them needs to build a community in his or her class. Right?" I probed.

"Yes, we've been trying to do that, but we haven't gotten many people to take responsibility. It has been frustrating."

As soon as the words came out of this mouth, he realized what he was saying. He laughed, "Well, Brother Scott, I see what you mean. I need to work with our teachers to help them get a vision for selecting the right people to shepherd the folks in their classes. Okay, it took me a minute, but I've got it now." Richard chuckled, and we laughed with him.

I turned to Joel. When we made eye contact, he tried not to glare at me. I asked, "So Joel, what are your plans? Who are your five key people going to be?" I could tell it was killing him to talk in the meeting at all, and it was especially galling for him to watch everybody else get so excited about the next step in our plans. He took a second, and then he answered, "I've got five people. No problem."

For the sake of the group, I didn't think it was a good idea to probe too much at that point. I just said, "Great. I think it will help everybody to pick well."

I was encouraged by their initial impressions in considering the "who" for each team, but I was well aware that the "when" was just as important. We would need to be creative and flexible in finding the right times to meet in order to impart heart and skills. Some team members were available most of the time, but others would have a hard time finding a consistent time to meet.

> We would need to be creative and flexible in finding the right times to meet in order to impart heart and skills.

I shared my concerns about the need for consistency and flexibility, explaining that there would be no cookie-cutter answers, no one-size-fits-all. Then I invited discussion. Brittany's team was really two separate teams: one comprised of women who didn't work outside the home and met during the day once every two or three weeks, and the other of career women who met for thirty minutes before the evening women's Bible study. Justin's group of young adults usually had difficulty finding a time that was convenient for everybody, but he was committed to try harder. Dan's student ministry had recently started meeting with volunteers during one of the worship hours every Sunday morning. His top leadership team, though, met every other Sunday night at his house for planning and prayer.

I wasn't concerned about the exact time and place our staff team members met with their ministry teams. I just wanted to have the conversation, wrestle with the complexities, and determine solutions that worked best for each team. A few could meet weekly, but some could only find time only once a month. Some met during the day, some at night, and some during church services. I didn't care how they resolved the problem. It might not be easy, but it was necessary to find the best time for the most leaders.

We had covered *who* and *when*. Now it was time to talk about *how*. I asked, "What content are you going to impart to your top five (or seven or however many) people this year? I don't expect you to ask them to do all we did last year, but they still need to commit themselves to filling their hearts with truth, grace, and leadership principles so they can pour themselves into others. What do you think?"

Most of the people on their teams had families and full-time jobs. We talked about what would stretch them without being so demanding that it would discourage them. We had a great discussion during which they concluded that they would ask team members to read five books and listen to twelve messages.

Mark asked, "How will they pick the books and messages? You let us pick ours. Should we let them pick theirs?"

"Great question," I replied, "although I think it might good for you to look at your list from last year and select the titles that were most helpful for them to read and hear. Be sure to include a variety of spiritual inspiration, general leadership, and topics pertaining to your particular ministry. How does that sound?"

Mark suggested, "What if we assign four and ten, and let them choose one book and two CDs on their own?"

Everybody was nodding. "Great idea. Let's go with that. You can cover one book each quarter—those are the four you pick—and one will be a wild card."

As a summary of our discussion so far, I told them, "I want you to come to next week's staff meeting with your plan for equipping your team this year. It needs to include who your top five people are (or will be, if you need to make some changes), when you will meet with them, and the list of books and CDs for them this year. Are you good with that?" They nodded.

I continued, "And a year from today, I'm going to ask all of you for a report of how your team pro-gressed this year. Got it?"

Yes, they got it. Justin asked, "What about us? Are we going to read books and listen to CDs this year, or are we done with that?"

> We still have to feed our souls so we become even better models. I expect you to read books and listen to messages for the rest of your life.

"We still have to feed our souls so we become even better models. I expect you to read books and listen to messages for the rest of your life. But this year, I want to set our goals. I hope that's okay with you. This year, I want you to read twelve books and listen to fifty-two messages."

Several of them looked perplexed. They had come that day expecting to do more, not less. I explained, "Last year we jump-started our efforts to be the leaders God wants us to be. This year the focus is on sustainability."

A few of them looked genuinely disappointed, so I continued, "Hey, I'm not letting you off easy. Not by a long shot. You've proven that you are learners, and now equipping is going to be hard work. You're going to have to be more like Paul—a 'nursing mother' tenderly caring for the people on your ministry teams. Equipping people was hard work for Jesus, and it's hard work for us as well. Jesus gave everything for His followers, for the lost people He met, and for us. He's not asking us for anything less. He wants us to give everything we've got for Him and His kingdom!" (I almost started preaching again at this point, but I reined it in—well, almost. I got a few looks like, "There he goes again." But that's okay. I'm used to it.)

"And this time next year, I'm going to ask you to bring your list of twelve books and fifty-two CDs along with your report about your team." I thought they should know that, but I was learning to clearly state my expectations.

A Few Questions

Dave had been thinking. "About the books and messages for our teams and for us . . . What if we want our teams to go over books and CDs we covered last year? I guess those don't count this year, huh?"

I asked, "Are you going to teach them to your team?"

"Yeah, four books."

"Are you going to read them again?"

"Of course. I have to be prepared if I'm going to lead our team in the discussion."

"Then I don't have any problem with your reading a few books again. Heck, I read a few great books over and over again. I can't get enough of them."

Dave realized again that my goal isn't numbers at all. I'm more than willing to be flexible when I see that people are sold out to the cause.

At that moment, I realized that I hadn't even mentioned another important point. I said, "Hey, I don't know how you've been leading your team meetings, but if we're going to pour heart and skills into those we work with, we need to make sure our meetings reflect our commitments."

Justin asked, "What exactly do you mean?"

"In the past year, have our staff meetings changed?"

Justin answered, "Yeah, we've spent more time talking about the principles we're learning than we did before—which was little to none."

I might have taken offense to that last little comment . . . if it hadn't been true. I continued, "So you're going to need to change your team meetings, too. The content of your meetings should reflect your priority to develop multiplying disciples."

> The content of your meetings should reflect your priority to develop multiplying disciples.

"So," Dave was thinking out loud, "about half inspiration and teaching and half administration?"

"That sounds about right. Be flexible, but don't forget that our priority, our core value of leadership, is to build leaders into multipliers. Think about the past year. Our weekly discussions have been the richest we've ever had. That's what you want to establish with your teams. Remember, it's not about your doing the work of the ministry. Those days are over. And it's not about getting others to do the work you don't want to do. That's not real leadership. What we're working toward is enflaming hearts and imparting skills so people on your team will be thrilled God is using them to change the world."

I stopped for a second, and then I asked a question that just came to mind: "What do you expect to happen on your teams this year? How do you think your people will respond? What difference will it make?"

Brittany said, "I think they'll love it!"

Dan replied, "They're going to get what we got last year. They're going to grow, and they're going to become better leaders."

Justin was thinking about the elephant in the room. He was diplomatic enough not to say anything directly about Joel, but everybody knew that's what he was thinking. He calmly predicted, "I'll probably find out that a few of my people don't want to go where the rest of us are going."

He had spoken the hard truth. Jesus personally selected His closest followers, yet one of them betrayed Him, and all of them ran away when He was arrested. Nobody had to say a word after Justin spoke, but we all were suddenly aware that it would be foolish to expect 100 percent success.

"Scott," Justin finally said after a long silence, "what do we do when somebody on the team says 'no'—either at the beginning or later in the year?"

"What do you think?" I asked the group.

Mark said, "We'd better select well from the beginning."

And Dan jumped in, "And we need a plan for how to deal with people who don't make it—for any reason."

I told them, "I made a mistake last year by not asking you more often how you were doing with your reading and listening. I should have done a better job of keeping up with you so I could offer assistance.

Don't delay like I did. Ask more often, assume less, and stay on top of your teams—not to micromanage them, but to encourage them. I'll do a better job of that this year, too."

As they absorbed all that was being said, I saw the same range of reactions I had seen a year before: most were eager to go, but a few were more cautious. They weren't sure if they fully grasped the whole strategy, and they lacked confidence they could equip people on their teams to become multipliers.

I realized a few of them needed a pep talk. "Look, you proved to me last year that you are fully committed to the Lord to be all He wants you to be. I couldn't ask for anything more. I know I'm asking some of you to do things you've never done before. That's why we're allotting three years to change our culture. I expect you to have questions, and I expect some of the people you select to come up short. That's life, and it's the nature of ministry. You can select and train as well as you possibly can, but there's still going to be a dropout or two. Stay focused, and be tenacious. I'm not going to jump on any of you because somebody on your team fails. If that happens—*when* that happens—we will find someone else to take his or her place. In fact, you might go ahead and have somebody in mind to step in, or you may want to start with six or seven people so you will be sure to end the year with five champions on your team. Does that make sense?"

> You can select and train as well as you possibly can, but there's still going to be a dropout or two.

They didn't say a word, but I could see that my explanation helped fill in some of the blanks. They knew there would be more questions as the year went along about replacing people who dropped out. I had one more thought. I told them, "The most powerful thing you can say to those you are equipping is how God has been using this process to change *your* life. Tell them about our conversation last year, and share the hopes and fears you experienced during the year. Talk about how God used the books, the messages, our staff team discussions, and your talks with others to inspire you. Tell them about the tangible and intangible benefits you've experienced. And then say, 'That's what I want for you.' They will understand that these aren't just hoops you want them to jump through. They're habits of a lifetime to quench our thirst for God, and they equip us to make a huge difference by developing generations of leaders. I think they'll get the picture."

I could tell Dave wanted to say something. I asked, "Dave, what's going on? What are you thinking?"

He took a deep breath, and then he said softly, "Scott, it has been really great this past year, and I'm fully on board with our plan for next year. But a few people on this team are miles ahead of me. Dan has a great leadership team and tons of terrific volunteers. They are multiplying like crazy. And Brittany . . . man, she's awesome at building leaders. You could tell her to stop and she would keep going strong. Nothing's going to get in her way."

I had a bead on Dave's real question. "And you want to know how it's going to look if you try like crazy but you don't see the same kind of results. Is that it?"

"Exactly. And what if the few people on my team want to leave and be part of the student ministry or the women's ministry? That's what I'm afraid of."

"Dave, I really appreciate your honesty. You make a great point. Some of us are leading areas of ministry that are really exciting, and multitudes of sharp folks want to join us. But some of us are in roles that are more administrative. There are several things I would say. First, we need to be honest about a tendency to compare ourselves or our ministries to others, because our ambition should be to please God rather than compete with fellow believers. And second, leadership is based on the powerful combination of respect and relationship. As we model a life of dedication to Christ and integrity in our work, we will earn respect. As we care for people, share their hopes and hurts, and learn to listen with compassion, we

> Leadership is based on the powerful combination of respect and relationship.

will build strong relationships. Most of the people you choose to be your five already know that we've ramped up so we can be better leaders. Now you can look each of them in the eye and say, 'Pastor Scott asked me to pray and ask God for wisdom to choose five people to train as leaders who equip others. Will you be one of the people on my team?' I can imagine people feeling incredibly honored to join you. If you're doing those things, I'll live with the results. How's that?"

"Sounds good," Dave replied with a relieved smile.

I had another flash of insight. "In fact, I think it would be great for you to sit down with the five people you select, and in your first conversation ask, 'How many people can our children's ministry (or young adults or students or senior adults or women's ministry or worship, or media arts) lead?' And let them answer. Do you remember our conversation about that?" They nodded. "Let them wrestle with it, and then go through the same process we talked about: the leaky bucket, three kinds of people on our teams, the goal, the steps to help people reach the goal . . . all that. And then tell them you want them to soak up all the leadership principles, grace, and truth their hearts can hold so they can become great models to the people on their teams. Explain that our church goal is 1,000, so each ministry has to expand its capacity. Everybody has to grow. That's the kind of conversation I want you to have with your five. Can you do that?"

Mark answered for the group, "No problem."

Joel finally joined the conversation. He asked, "Are we expecting these people to pay for their books and CDs?"

"That's a great question." I tried to hide my surprise at Joel's sudden involvement. I hadn't thought about it, but I told them, "The church will pay for the four books you pick for your teams. Your people can pay for their wild card picks. I think your team can come up with a dozen free, or almost free, messages to listen to, so that shouldn't be a problem. Joel, does that sound fair?"

He wasn't quite smiling, but he said, "Yeah. Fair enough."

"One more question," Richard spoke up. "Uh, this year, we, uh, had a party, and you, uh . . . "

"And I gave you a check for $500."

"Yes, you certainly did!"

"And that's what's going to happen again next year. When you bring the report of your ministry team and your own list of books and CDs, I'll hand you a check for $500 and we'll party all day and have a great dinner to celebrate what God has done."

Richard grinned, "I was hoping you'd say that."

I said slowly, with as much mock drama as I could muster, "And if you don't do it . . ."

Almost in unison, several of them said, "We'll have to stay behind and spend ten minutes telling you why we should stay on staff."

"Because," I grinned, "you've got to grow . . ."

Several of them responded immediately, ". . . or you have to go!"

Justin looked at Joel. He held his hands up and said, "Hey, I've been there, and it ain't pretty. I'm not going there again." We had a good laugh, but everybody knew I was serious.

"One more thing," I told them as the meeting ended. "Last year some of you needed some help but didn't ask for it soon enough, which caused some frustration. This year I want you to know that I'm here for you anytime you need help. As you start to coach your five, I'm going to be coaching you. Ask me anything at any time. This year we're turning an important corner, and I'll do everything I can do to help you. Got it?"

They all nodded. I suspected they would need more help than they did last year, but I felt confident they would be more willing to ask for it this time. I prayed for our efforts to select and equip the ministry teams, and then I told them, "I'll see you next week. Don't forget to bring a list of your five people, the four books and twelve messages for them, and the twelve books and fifty-two CDs for you. And before you go, let me pray again to thank God for you."

My prayer of thanks came from an overflowing heart. We had made incredible progress in only one year. I was sure we would keep going strong in the next twelve months.

After they left, I was pumped! When planning for this meeting, I had been hopeful that they would buy into the strategy for the year. They had—even better than I had hoped.

Dan's Response to the Second Conversation

During the three years, Dan Hunter was the student pastor

at The Oaks. He now serves as Lead Pastor at

Living Church in Mansfield, Texas.

For years, I had read and taught Paul's instruction to leaders to equip people for the work of the ministry, but as the second year started, I finally had real handles on what that looks like. The first year was terrific for me, and I was excited about launching into the second year. I had learned a lot, but it hadn't been easy. When the first year started, I didn't know how I would cram all the reading and listening into my schedule. (I wondered if I needed to take a year or two off from marriage to make it work, but thankfully, it didn't come to that.) By the end of the year, though, the discipline of learning had become a habit—a really good habit.

When Scott asked us to invest our lives in five people during the coming year, I mentally scrolled through the leaders I worked with. The student ministry involved a lot of excited people, but I wanted to choose wisely. I wondered if all five would make it through the year, so I picked seven.

In our initial conversation we talked about the *who*, *when*, and *how* of our strategy that year, but I wanted to emphasize the *why*. Scott had made it clear that our goal wasn't to get people to read books and listen to messages. Those were means to an end, not the end itself. We wanted to create a new mindset among our key people. We desired to equip them, inspire them, and help them do all God was calling them to do. The reading and listening requirements were just a part of that vision. I realized that my role had changed. Previously I had organized my volunteers to help me be the hero of our student ministry, but now I was going to equip a bunch of heroes.

To be honest, I had serious concerns about a couple of people on our staff team. We had all had some difficulty during the first year, but a couple of people had really struggled. (I was pretty sure one of them hadn't told the truth about the books and messages he had completed, but it wasn't up to me to call him out.) Now they would have to step up their game and develop leaders. I didn't think they would be able to do it, and I didn't know how Scott would respond. It was going to be an interesting year.

I desperately wanted to be an equipper. I knew the previous year had been essential preparation for the role I wanted to play. The number of books and talks we chose would challenge but not overwhelm our five to seven leaders. We wanted them to love our conversations about what they were learning, so we gave them very reachable goals.

When we left the meeting that day, I was fired up. I was going to pour myself into people who would soak up leadership principles like they were sponges!

Think about it . . .

1. What kind of preparation did Scott do for this meeting? What plans were in concrete? Which ones were flexible?

2. How did he help everyone turn the corner from filling their hearts so they could be good models to a plan for equipping specific people?

3. How did Scott and his team answer the questions *who, when,* and *how?*

4. How would you have answered Dave's question about the danger of comparison?

5. Joel didn't cause any problem in this meeting, but he could have been a huge distraction. How would you have handled it if he had become a problem?

6. How reasonable was the plan for the second year? If you had been Scott, what would your expectations have been when the staff walked out the door that day?

Chapter 5

The Events of the Second Year: Who, When, and How?

During the week following the second conversation, I watched carefully to gauge the mood of the team. Most of them had already seen dramatic results in their relationships with people on their ministry teams, but they realized this was a different challenge. They now had to be sure they were preparing the right people, not simply recruiting warm bodies and nice Christians. I overheard serious conversations in the hall about various choices for team members. They asked each other for advice, and they listened intently.

The Next Staff Meeting

When they filed into my office to give me their plans for the year, a new sensation was in the air. It was hard to put my finger on it, but it seemed to be a blend of excitement and fear, much like I feel when I attempt something new and crazy like rock climbing. Even when it's something I'm sure I want to do (especially if I'm doing it with my friends), I'm scared to death that I'll fall or look like a fool.

As each person handed me the list of people, books, and CDs, I asked him or her to tell the group the thought process that went into making the list. Some of the group had never wavered from the five to seven people whose names they jotted down the week before, but a few of them had wrestled long and hard with their selections. During the week they realized they had been riding the wrong horses. In only a week, they had to reassess their teams. Making personnel changes after they have been selected is always a hundred times harder than doing due diligence before choosing them. A few were struggling with their previous choices, the reality of hard conversations to come, and the uncertainty that they would make better selections this time.

Mark had figured out how to put three bands together, each with someone in charge. Since he led the existing band, the people he chose were the two leaders of the other bands, two guys working the soundboard, and a lady who helped him with administrative details. "That's my team," he announced, "and I can't believe it took me so long to put this together. Having two additional bands will help relieve pressure, and it will be great to have the sound guys and an administrator meeting with us to coordinate everything."

I asked, "Who will you have in the other two bands?"

He laughed, "That's not a problem. We've had dozens of people ask if they could play or sing in our band, but we haven't had a place for them. Now we can have three times as many people involved. We're scheduling auditions for the other two bands in the next couple of weeks."

"Fantastic!"

Most of the group had struggled with a time to meet with their teams. Dan was already meeting regularly to equip and encourage a large team of volunteers, but now he realized he needed to carve out time to devote to his top leaders to help them lead *their* teams of volunteers more effectively. The staff team discovered that scheduling meetings wasn't an exact science. What worked for one didn't work for another, yet they all had to find a consistent schedule and place to meet with their top five members.

The conversations with everyone on the team helped many of them crystallize their thinking. For example, Richard had said, "I can't meet with my teachers every week like Dan does with his volunteers. It just won't work."

"No problem," I assured him. "When can you meet so that it works for all of you?"

> What worked for one didn't work for another, yet they all had to find a consistent schedule and place to meet with their top five members.

His frustrations had been building all week, and now they spilled out. He said again, "I don't see how we can do it every week."

"How about once a month? Can you find a time to meet that often?"

Richard looked like a load had been lifted from his back. "Yes. Yes, I think we can certainly do that. Maybe we can have breakfast one Saturday morning a month."

"That'll work."

Brittany had been having two leadership meetings, one for women who didn't have careers outside the home, and one for working women. "I'd love to have them meet together every time," she said, "but that's not going to happen. We'll keep having two separate meetings with leaders, but I'd like to get them all together at least once a quarter from now on. It would be extremely helpful to have everybody together for a united vision at least a few times each year."

"That's cool!"

When I got to Dave, he told the group, "My list of leaders is a little different than I expected it to be. As I prayed this week, I sensed God leading me to replace one person in a key position."

Dave was very serious, but Mark almost laughed, "Yeah, I know exactly who it is! Heck, I could have told you that you needed to replace her." Dave looked surprised, but then he smiled, "I guess I'm the last one to figure it out, huh?"

We all enjoyed the moment. I asked, "Dave, have you chosen someone else?"

"Sure did. It's Suzanne, and I've already talked to her. I've got to tell you, she was so excited about this role. I think she's going to do a terrific job. To be honest, I don't think I would ever have made the change if we hadn't talked about asking God for direction to pick five for this year."

I was thrilled to hear Dave's report, but I could tell Joel was frustrated. When I got to him, he almost barked, "Scott, this just doesn't apply to me. I don't have five people, and besides, we don't need leaders in media arts."

His statement contained more than a hint of sarcasm, but I decided to overlook it and try to be helpful. "I know your area of ministry isn't just like the others, but all of us can build leaders more effectively." I walked up to the whiteboard and asked him, "What are the primary functions you perform and the people you have now?"

The lasers coming out of his eyes could have brought down an intercontinental ballistic missile. Clearly, he didn't want to process his plans in front of the others, but I wasn't willing to give him a free pass. He didn't say a word, so I wrote on the board: *Photography, Video, Brochures.* "Those are your main areas, aren't they?" Still not a sound. I continued, "And you currently have six volunteers who help you fairly consistently." I wrote their names on the board. "It looks to me that you have your team. Now you just need a plan to equip them. If you have the right person in charge of photography, that person could have a bunch of people taking pictures we could use. Videos take the most time and expertise. It would help to have somebody in charge who has a team of people for scheduling shoots, lighting, sound, shooting the footage, and editing."

"I do all that now," he said through clenched teeth.

"Wouldn't it be great to have a team helping you?" I didn't wait for an answer—or a protest. I had made my point, and I didn't want to get bogged down in an argument at that point. I said only, "Let's talk later about all this." Without missing a beat, I moved on to the last person, Dan. I figured I could count on him to end the reports on a high note, and he didn't let me down.

As each person went over the list of who would be on the ministry team, when they would meet, and the books and messages they had chosen, I asked some simple but important questions: "Which books will you cover with your team?" "Which chapters will you go over each time you meet?" "Who is going to lead the discussions?" The first person was a little surprised by how specific I wanted him to be, but by the time he was finished, all the rest had their plans in place. They knew I wasn't going to skip anybody.

In spite of Joel's resistance and the concerns of a couple of others, I wanted to provide a bigger picture of what to expect during the year. When they finished their reports, I began, "This is fantastic! You've done great work this week. I know some of you have really wrestled with picking your top five. Working with people who have leadership abilities is often a thrill, but it can also be messy, awkward, and confusing. Some of the people on your teams will be right with you most of the time. Others will go to the same meetings and hear the same vision, and you can pour your heart into them and impart the life of Christ to them, and they will still look at you like you're speaking Swahili. We may have clear plans and processes, but people aren't electronics or machines. They're people!"

Most of my listeners smiled and a few of them nodded as I continued. "Think about the 'leaders' in the Bible. Saul was considered a slam dunk, but he failed miserably. David was the one of the greatest leaders of all time, but he failed morally and needed a friend to confront him about his sin. And think of Jesus and His disciples. I can imagine Him shaking His head day after day. He was the perfect model of humility, strength, and truth, but even after three years His 'top twelve' argued about who was the greatest. And they ran away when He needed them most. Are your people any different? Are *you and I* any different?"

"So," Justin asked, "what are you saying? What can we expect from the people on our teams?"

"You can expect a range of responses. It's crucial that you select well, but even when you do, you probably won't avoid disappointment. In some cases you'll see signs along the way and have advance warning, but a few problems will seem to come out of nowhere."

Dan spoke up, "And that's why you suggested we might want to start with seven people in order to end the year with five star players."

"Exactly." Realistic expectations are important, so I wanted

> As we build strong relationships with the people we're equipping, some incredible things happen.

to explain one more point. "As we build strong relationships with the people we're equipping, some incredible things happen. When they're convinced we really care about them and aren't just using them to do what we don't want to do, they open up to us. They share concerns about their marriages (if they're married) or their girlfriend or boyfriend (if they're single). They open up about their hopes and fears, and they ask for advice about the things that matter most to them. They may ask you how to do things that you thought they already understood. They may ask you how to pray, how to hear God, how to study the Bible, and how to handle sexual temptations. They may have been in church for twenty years without anyone ever helping them with those foundational aspects of walking with God. They will talk to you about how to raise kids, how to manage a difficult person at work, how to comfort a parent who has cancer, and a hundred other things that really count."

I looked around the room. They were all really tracking with me—even Joel. I reminded them, "Paul told the Thessalonians that he didn't just tell them the truth; he imparted his own life to them because they had become dear to him. I'll tell you, caring for people and leading them with love and purpose is the most meaningful, most deeply satisfying thing you can do on this earth. It's not about a person managing a soundboard (I looked at Mark) or teaching a class (I looked at Richard) or taking care of snotty little kids during church (I looked at Dave). It's about the privilege of being partners with men and women (I looked at everybody in the room) on the adventure of changing the world together."

Yeah, I know. I was preaching again, and I wasn't finished. "Think about what has been happening this past year and what is going to happen this year. As all seven of you pour your lives into at least five people, you'll be equipping thirty-five key leaders in our church. I'm working with nine on our board and the seven of you, so we'll have fifty-two people who are being equipped, loved, challenged, and directed to be all they can be for Christ and His kingdom."

I paused for a second, and then I reminded them of where we were going. "Remember that this year isn't the end of our goal. Selection is important now because the people we equip this year need to have the capacity to equip their own five next year." I drew a diagram on the board of our team with five lines coming from each person, and

> Selection is important now because the people we equip this year need to have the capacity to equip their own five next year.

then with five coming from each of those. I asked, "You haven't forgotten that, have you?"

They smiled as if to say, "No, you've pummeled us with that concept pretty well. We haven't forgotten it." But they also realized that we were very much in process. The plans they had submitted in our staff meeting that day weren't about books and CDs; they were about flesh and blood people with hopes and dreams, desires to please God, and normal, human temptations to turn their backs on Him. Selecting and equipping leaders was going to be a lot harder than reading and listening to messages. Most of them could tell, though, that I was tenacious and flexible—tenacious about the goal of becoming multipliers and flexible about the means to achieve that goal. They could expect a lot of mid-course adjustments along the way.

Mark asked a pertinent question, "Scott, how do I launch this with my five people? I can't figure out what to say without it sounding like I just made all this up."

"Great question." I stalled for a few seconds to come up with a great answer. "Here's what I would do if I were you. I would walk into the first meeting with them and tell them our story of last year. I would tell them how I challenged you to be a good role model, and how you now want to equip them to be leaders. You can say, 'Pastor Scott asked us to do this—and you know what Pastor Scott is like; he's intense—and I want to help you the way he helped me last year.' How does that sound?"

"I can do that," Mark said confidently.

Some people had come to the meeting with an airtight plan for the year, but most had learned a thing or two during our discussion. They were going to make some immediate changes to the plans they had submitted that morning. I wasn't sure, though, if Joel was on board at all.

The Next Day

I didn't want to let too much time pass before meeting with Joel about his plans for the year. I saw he was in his office the day after our staff meeting, so I went to his door and asked, "Hey, got a minute?"

He looked up from his computer and his expression instantly changed from a smile to a frown. "I guess this is where you fire me, huh?"

"No, this is where we talk about your goals."

"Great," he said sarcastically as he pushed his chair back and crossed his arms. "Bring it on."

"Joel, I know you're frustrated, but I want you to know that I really want you to succeed. I'll do anything I can to help you." I could tell I wasn't making much of a dent in his defensiveness, but I was determined to give it my best shot. "This is the direction God is leading our church and our staff team. Some people on the team have roles that are fully focused on building people, and some of you are in roles that are more creative or administrative. All of us, though, can learn to build people who can build more people. It's different for Brittany than it is for Dave in the children's ministry. And it's different for Justin than it is for Richard. I think we've made it clear that we all have to be flexible in finding a way to make it work, but we aren't going to back away from our goal of building multipliers." I paused for a few seconds, and then I asked, "Is there anything about this you want to push back on?"

"No." A two-letter answer was all he was willing to give.

"Then I need to know: are you in?"

He shrugged his shoulders, and finally he said, "Yeah, I guess so. I don't see how it can work, but I'm willing to give it a try."

The level of Joel's enthusiasm was underwhelming, but I decided to take his words at face value. "Okay. I think it would be good for you to take another look at your plan. You can give it to me next week before staff meeting. Can I help you?"

"No," he said without looking up. "I've got it."

"Great." I walked out, knowing that unless God did a major work in Joel's life, it was going to be a long, difficult year—for both of us.

Three Months Later

I didn't want to make the same mistake I had made the first year: assuming that people would make things work on their own and waiting too long to check on them. So during the first three months of the second year, I followed up with each person regularly. By and large I was excited about their progress, and I was glad that they saw me as an ally this year. Many of them dropped by my office to ask advice about this problem or that opportunity.

At the three-month mark, however, I wanted to get clear reports from each person. When they came to the next staff meeting I said, "We've been intentionally equipping ministry teams for three months. This morning I would like us all to describe how it's going for our teams."

As I expected, some of them were as pumped as ever about what God was doing in them and through them. Their ministry teams were having life-changing conversations about the principles they were reading, and those people were modeling lives of integrity and excellence to even more people. The vision of building multipliers was cascading down to more generations, and it was thrilling to hear the stories!

But as I anticipated, others were struggling. One said sadly, "My team started strong, but in the past few weeks it seems like they're just checking off boxes. They have lost their passion." Another commented, "I'm having trouble keeping people motivated. They are volunteers. If they don't do their assignments, I can't threaten them by telling them I'll fire them. I need to find a way to keep them excited for the right reasons." And another said simply, "Scott, I'm not you. I don't have this vision thing down like you do."

I appreciated their honesty, and I reminded them that we had talked about the complexity of leading people. It was a great time to reinforce things we had talked about many times before, but to drive the point deeper because the things they had discussed a year ago had now become very real to them.

I said, "I don't want you to be me, but maybe you can take a piece of me and a piece of two or three other leaders to create your own motivational style. Every time you meet with your team, talk about how God has used the books and messages in your life. Tell them about particular things you've learned and how God used a principle in your marriage, with your kids, or in your ministry. Assure them, like I have assured you a dozen times, that our goal isn't to put checkmarks on a list. Our goal isn't to convince others to do something they don't want to do. Our goal is to transform our hearts, to enflame our love for Jesus, and to sharpen our skills so we become the best leaders we can be. And then we want to inspire others to love God with all their hearts and devote themselves to His cause with every ounce of energy and excellence."

I looked around to be sure they were tracking with me, and then I said, "If we're inspiring others with a God-sized vision and with Christ's heart of love, they will *want* to read books and listen to messages because they will be energized by the hope of partnering with God to fulfill the greatest mission on earth. The win isn't the lists you turned in three months ago. The win is changed lives."

I had said almost exactly the same thing many different ways during the past fifteen months, but now they were using the principles they had learned and needed to hear with a new set of ears. They were developing a commitment to apply the truths they had learned, not just soak them in. As usual, I was gearing up to preach. I told them, "Folks, you and I can't coast on what we achieved last year. Yeah, we had a great year, but it was just a start. We have to keep drinking in the love and power of God, and we need to be challenged from the hairs on our heads to our socks to see God use us to change lives. I believe God gave us this three-year plan to grow from workers to equippers to multipliers, but we're not machines. We have to stay fresh in our walks with Him, and we have to keep learning and applying leadership principles. We can't give away something we don't own." They needed this reminder, and I always do, too.

I wasn't quite finished. I told them, "When Jesus was with the disciples, He didn't just talk about the job that needed to be done. When they walked together or sat around campfires, I'm sure they talked about whatever was on the disciples' hearts. Those things were important to Jesus precisely because they were important to His friends. The people on your team aren't cogs in your ministry machine. They're people with hurts and hopes, fears and delights. Find out what thrills them, what causes them to lie awake at night, and what they long to become. You don't have to provide all the answers to their questions. They just need to know they matter to you—not as production units, but as friends."

I sensed that people on the team felt relieved and stimulated by our discussion that morning. The next few months would be pivotal, and a few of them needed to make significant changes in the way they related to their teams.

Six Months After the Conversation

Three months later it was time for another checkup. One morning in staff meeting I asked for an update of how it was going with their ministry teams. Again, some reported amazing progress. Mark said that his two other bands had come together, which was no surprise since they had already played during worship a few times. Brittany had made a few minor shifts among her top leadership team in the women's ministry, and she was excited about the maturity and enthusiasm of the new leaders. Dave had the same team in children's ministry, but he was building them up like never before.

Many of the staff, though, were discovering that certain people they thought had been potential leaders weren't working out as well as they had expected. Justin told us about a young man he felt would be a key leader in the young adult ministry for years to come who had "hit a ceiling." I asked what he meant, and he told us, "He was fine with coming to our leadership meetings last year and was quick to offer his input, but when I asked him to go beyond being an advisor, he dragged his feet. He didn't say, 'No, I'm not going to become a leader who equips others and multiplies,' but his reluctance is obvious. I've tried everything I know to motivate him. I've poured my guts out, but nothing makes a dent."

Dan chimed in, "Yeah, I've had one disappointment, but I've also seen another lady take far more responsibility than I thought she ever would. I've been amazed by how much she has done for the volunteers she leads. I'd like to clone her!"

"It's always a mixed bag," I reminded them. "We shouldn't be surprised. When Jesus said, 'Follow me,' some people did, but others walked away and left Him standing in the road. Even His closest followers had their bad moments. One betrayed Him; one denied Him three times; all of them deserted Him in His grief and loneliness. Not everybody on our teams is going to be a Peter, James, or John. Some will be, and we treasure them . . . but even they may let us down from time to time. Other team members will be faithful but unspectacular, and some will hurt us deeply, like Judas betrayed Jesus and Demas walked out on

Paul. The question isn't whether or not we will experience disappointments in leading people, but how well we anticipate them and respond to them when they happen."

Justin asked, "Why didn't that guy just tell me from the beginning that he wasn't interested? I think I was pretty clear about the commitment."

> When Jesus said, "Follow me," some people did, but others walked away and left Him standing in the road. Even His closest followers had their bad moments.

"Great question." I turned to the group. "Why do you think people hang on for weeks or months before they—or we—realize it's not going to work?"

Several people offered their suggestions, but Brittany gave the best answer: "Maybe they're testing us to see if we really mean what we say. They've probably heard plenty of people before who didn't demand accountability, and they may have thought we would be the same way."

"Yeah," Mark summarized this part of our conversation. "They're testing us while we're testing them."

Everybody seemed to like this answer. But I cautioned them, "Don't assume that everyone who walks away is betraying you or sinning against God. People may be in a particular season of life with good reasons not to commit to your ministry. Think of a woman who just had a child, or someone completely invested in a civic group who sees it as a mission field, or someone who gets a new job and has to move away or spend more time at work. Those choices are not wrong or sinful. We need to affirm people who are following Christ with their whole hearts, wherever He leads them."

"What you're saying is that I shouldn't demonize the guy who leaves my team because he got a job in Atlanta?" Justin said with a grin.

"Probably not," several people replied.

"So," I returned to the previous point, "think about your team members. Who is your Peter, James, and John? I hope you don't have a Judas, but you may well have some people like the rich young ruler or Simon the Pharisee who expressed a desire to connect with Jesus but bailed when they didn't like what they heard."

We had a wonderful discussion about the reality of what was going on with their teams. It got personal pretty quickly, so I reminded them that we were committed to confidentiality. For the rest of the morning—and for the rest of the year—the people on our team seemed to have more realistic expectations about their team members. They tried harder to touch hearts and motivate their teams, and they were less frustrated or angry when someone didn't follow through with commitments.

A few of them also realized that some of the people they had selected weren't going to make it. Unless they added one or two solid people to their ministry teams, they wouldn't finish the year with five strong people. A few hard conversations took place that week to remove certain team members, but those were countered by other challenging, inspiring talks to invite new people to join teams.

The End of the Year

A couple of weeks before the year's final meeting, I reminded our staff that they needed to bring their lists of the five people they were equipping, the books and messages they had used with their teams, and the list of twelve books and fifty-two messages they had chosen for personal development. I said, "I'm looking forward to handing you a check and having fun all day! Be sure to wear casual clothes." Everybody but Joel looked excited.

When the day arrived, they assembled with more than the usual banter and kidding. I told them, "I'm so proud of you! All year I've watched you wrestle with selecting the right people, making necessary adjustments, and pouring yourselves into their lives to equip them to lead. I've heard from lots of people who told me how much you've meant to them this year, and I believe them. Your teams have grown spiritually and in their abilities to lead. And in case you haven't noticed, the church has grown, too. We're up to almost 900! Two years ago when we started this plan, we were at about 650. The church has been at the 900 level before, but this time we're not going to drop. We're going to keep growing because our foundation is strong. You and your teams are that foundation. Way to go!"

I had asked everyone to make copies of their reports to hand out, so one by one they passed out sheets and prepared to summarize their year. I didn't want them to talk about only books, talks, and numbers. I told them, "It's fine if you want to tell us about your list. But what I really want to hear is one story about how God changed somebody's life."

The reports were incredible! We had a blast hearing how God had prodded one young man to forgive his father, how a lady finally was honest about being sexually abused, and how several broken relationships were mended by God's grace through the honesty of a single courageous person. The life of Christ was being poured into the volunteers and staff on our teams, and more people were seeing God use them in amazing ways to teach, counsel, lead, and shepherd people throughout the church and the community. What we were doing was making a difference!

After each person's report, I presented a check for $500 as we all cheered. It was a lot of fun.

The last person to report was Joel. I hadn't seen any papers in his hand when he walked in. I hoped he had them under his chair or in his pocket, but I knew better than that. When I turned to him, he just shook his head in disgust—not at his failure, but because I had expected him to do something he didn't want to do. I had asked him several times during the last six months how he was doing with his team and with his twelve books and fifty-two messages. Each time he assured me, "No problem." Clearly it had been a ruse. He hadn't done anything all year.

I didn't yell or fuss or cuss. I just told the group. "Mark, if you'll bring the van up to the front, I'll meet the rest of you in a few minutes. Joel and I are going to have another talk."

They left the room without a sound and without delay. They may have wondered what I was going to say to Joel, but they didn't linger near the door to find out. When Joel and I were alone he told me, "Man, this just isn't my thing. I can't do it, and you shouldn't ask me to. It doesn't make any sense in my ministry area."

There was no need to argue. I told him, "You're right. It's not *your* thing, but it's *our* thing. It looks like you don't fit on our team, so we need to figure out what to do now."

He looked shocked, "What do you mean?"

I said, "What do you mean, 'What do you mean?' You just told me loud and clear that you're not on board with the goals and plans of our team." I took a deep breath. "I love you, Joel. I want you on the team, but you've proven that you don't want to be here. Other people have had questions. They asked them, got answers, and moved on. Other people have had struggles. They got help and found solutions."

His eyes were wide open now. "Scott, you're not going to fire me, are you?"

"I don't see it as me firing you. You've made the decision to leave our team on your own. That was your choice. You've resigned."

He tried to argue with me, but I told him, "I'm going to set up a meeting in a few days with you and Kim. We'll talk then."

He asked, "What are we going to talk about?"

I was incredulous. "What do you think we're going to talk about?"

"Well, you can't fire me."

I ignored his statement. "I'll call to let you know when we're going to meet."

He kept pressing me, asking if I was going to fire him. He said, "It's all about the stupid books and CDs, isn't it? Where did you come up with that, anyway?"

I looked him in the eye. "No, it's not about the books and CDs. It's about your life. For the past four years you have come to me over and over again, asking for help with projects because you didn't have enough bodies or the right people to help you get the job done. Many people are affected when you don't build a team. You suffer, the untrained people suffer, and I have suffered because I've had to miss other opportunities in order to bail you out so many times. You were part of a team that created a plan to resolve the problem, but then you didn't buy into it. That's the issue."

He wanted to debate the point, but I had already let this conversation go longer than it needed to. I held up my hand. "That's enough. We've talked about this for two years, and that's enough."

I stood up and said, "I'm going to go now and celebrate with the rest of the team. I'll let you know when we're meeting." On the way to the van I thought about what to say to the rest of the team, but I soon realized I didn't have to say a word. They had seen this day coming for a long time—even more clearly than I had. When I jumped into the van to head off to have a great day together, I let out a big cheer. It was as much angst as joy.

Bombs Away

I think it's best to explain at this point what happened with Joel. I met with our board to describe the situation and explain that Joel had, in effect, signaled his desire to resign by his consistent inaction during the past two years. To my utter surprise, they were shocked. I heard comments like, "We can't fire Joel. We need him." "He's such a great guy." "We love him and his family. You don't fire family, Scott!"

I spent three hours explaining that I wasn't firing him, but that's what they were hearing. I was startled by their disbelief and resistance. I hadn't anticipated anything but support from them.

I postponed my meeting with Joel for a few days while I wrestled with the board. I'm sure several of them called him to get his point of view, and it was a real struggle to help them see the situation from my perspective. The dialog was frustrating:

"Joel isn't organized."

"Yeah, but that's just Joel. He gets the job done, doesn't he?"

"No, he doesn't. You have no idea how many times he calls me to bail him out."

"And you don't want to help your staff?"

"Of course I want to help them, but if I have to do their work for them, that's 'assisted irresponsibility,' not leadership."

During those conversations, I realized nobody knew but me that I'd been propping Joel up for four years. This was a watershed moment for our board: were we going to do the convenient thing, or the right thing?

Finally, the board agreed that Joel's behavior had, indeed, constituted a resignation. With their begrudging support, I called Joel and asked him to bring Kim to my office the next morning. He was furious, "You're going to fire me? Is that what this meeting is about?"

I spoke calmly, but my guts were churning, "Bring Kim to my office tomorrow at ten o'clock. We'll talk then."

This meeting turned out to be even more of a bombshell than the board meeting had been. Before I even said a word, Kim accused me of betraying Joel, her, and their family. She hadn't come with a carefully reasoned statement. She was mad! I listened for a long time, but I was careful to refute several points along the way. When I told her that Joel and I had been talking about this for the past two years, she exploded.

"Talking about what? Nobody ever told me anything about leadership development. It doesn't relate to Joel's job anyway."

"Actually, it does." Obviously Joel hadn't told Kim about any of our plans, at least not from the point of view of the rest of the team. Now that she was caught completely off guard, she was defending her man to the death! I was fighting an uphill battle trying to explain everything that had happened, but I gave it my best shot.

After only a few sentences, she blurted out, "So you're firing Joel?"

"His unwillingness to participate in our staff's plans constitutes his resignation," I said calmly.

She stood up and glared at me, "We can go anywhere in the country we want to go!"

"I wanted you here," I told her. "I love you both, and I wanted Joel on our team."

Before I could say anything else, she took off for the door. She looked back and said, "You can't do this to us! We'll find a place a lot better than this!"

"Come back and sit down, Kim," I urged.

Her eyes tried to freeze me. "You're not my boss. You can't tell me what to do."

"Do you want Joel's severance? If you do, come back and sit down."

She stood for a long second or two, and then she returned and mumbled, "Whatever."

I went over the severance agreement with both of them. Joel would submit a letter of resignation. The church would provide several months' worth of salary with the stipulation that Joel and Kim were not to speak disparagingly of our team, the church, or me. And we planned a party at the church next week so everyone could thank them for their service.

During the week I met individually with each member of our staff to update everyone about what had happened. I didn't need to say a word. They all said essentially the same thing: "I knew it was coming, and frankly, I thought it would have been a year ago." I guess I'm a slow learner.

In addition to the staff and the board, I met with about seventy-five influential people in the church. I didn't go into all the details, but I wanted to inform them of Joel's resignation and answer questions. Those meetings were time consuming, but they were a wise investment of my time and energy. A potential crisis was averted by meeting with people, explaining the situation, and listening to them. Not a single person left the church because of Joel's and Kim's departure. I was convinced I had witnessed either a miracle or the results of our staff building strong relationships with people on their ministry teams throughout the church—or both.

Dan's Second Year

Leading volunteers is a lot different from working with staff members. My seven leaders were in college or had jobs, so they weren't available during the day. The challenge for me, then, was orchestrating my schedule to meet when they had free time—often early in the morning or after work. Every other week I met one-on-one with each person, and we got together as a team every other week as well. When we met, we didn't just talk about the content the team members were learning. We applied the principles to their lives and ministries.

For me the second year was significantly more difficult than the first year. It had been hard enough to carve out time to read books and listen to messages, but now I was adding another layer of time, effort, and complexity. When I met with my seven leaders, we had a ton to talk about, including their goals and dreams, their personal lives, and their ministries with students. As this was happening, I realized I *couldn't* be a worker any longer. I *had* to devote myself to equipping and releasing those people so they could touch far more lives than I could.

The eight of us decided on a schedule for reading the selected books. When we finished each one, we had a book review night with dinner and discussion. We went through each book chapter by chapter. They quickly realized they needed to underline or highlight important points, write notes in the margins, and answer the questions at the end of the chapters. We always ended each chapter by talking about the impact the concepts had on our lives. It was electric! Our conversations were so rich that it was hard to move to the next chapter. Our book review nights lasted about four hours and were highlights of my year.

Think about it . . .

1. How clearly did Scott articulate the need for each staff member to plan the *who, when,* and *how* of equipping five key leaders the second year? How clearly did the staff understand this plan? Explain your answer.

2. What might have been some causes of "vision leakage" between Scott's explanations to the staff and their explanations to their teams?

3. What concrete problems did the staff members face in selecting and equipping their top five leaders during this year?

4. How would you have helped them resolve those problems?

5. How did Scott try to keep the vision and motivation fresh? How would you have helped the staff in those areas?

6. How well did Scott handle the situation with Joel at the end of the year? How would you have handled it?

Chapter 6

Lessons Learned the Second Year: Staying Focused

Year two had been both thrilling and frustrating. Our team was making the transition from soaking up leadership principles to pouring them out to their individual ministry teams. It proved to be a messier process than I had expected, but overall it was a magnificent year of progress for everyone but Joel.

What follows are some important lessons I learned during the year.

The Necessity of Being a Role Model

I don't think we would have seen such success if I hadn't already been modeling what I asked my staff to do. Prior to the first conversation, I had spent years trying to equip leaders, train them in heart and skills, and help them become multipliers. God had transfused those values and practices deep in my bloodstream. I was a voracious reader, so it was easy for me to convince our staff of the benefits of reading tons of books and listening to countless messages because that's what I had been doing for years. And they knew it.

The staff never questioned my commitment to the cause, our goals, or the process of becoming great role models so we could equip people and build multipliers out of the abundance of God's grace in our hearts.

(They might have questioned my sanity from time to time, but not my integrity.)

In the first year, they jumped on board (all but one, anyway) because they had seen me reading, found me listening to great messages in my car, and heard me share stories and principles in almost every staff meeting and sermon. Now, in the second year, they again followed my example, this time by selecting key leaders and building them into multiplying disciples. They knew I wasn't asking them to do anything I wasn't already doing, and they knew I was committed to do it for the rest of my life.

For senior pastors, the process of the three conversations begins at least a year or so before he rolls it out to his staff. He has to prove—to himself as much as to them—that he has those leadership principles in his blood. If he tries to implement them before he has proven his integrity, they will disregard him when they hit a snag. What he says may be true, but they're looking as much at his example as his instructions.

> If a pastor wants his staff to bleed leadership development, he has to hemorrhage it!

Many senior pastors are gifted in important areas of ministry, such as Bible exposition, administration, and counseling. But if a pastor wants his staff to bleed leadership development, he has to hemorrhage it! He can't show up at the first conversation and tell the staff, "Hey, I'm just starting this, too." That won't work.

Jesus prayed all night before he picked His twelve. I should be willing to pray at least a few hours to ask God for wisdom in selecting the people I lead. In the second year when we turned the corner to actively select and equip teams of five, I was already working with sixteen people: nine on the board and our seven staff members.

In addition to those sixteen, every year I asked the Lord to lead me to an "eagle" I could pour my life into. That particular year, God put a man on my heart who was a successful businessman but had never been very active in the church. I was planning a mission trip to Belarus, and I asked him to join me. (He went home and told his wife that I had invited him on a trip to Bulgaria. Close enough.) He decided to go, and we had a blast together. We spent two weeks ministering to churches and helping pastors and laypeople. At various hours during the day we talked about his life and mine, his dreams and mine. We got to know each other very well. We discussed money, marriage, kids, work, and God's will for our lives. No topic was off-limits. We had such a great time together that we became good friends. He has gone with me on every subsequent trip to Belarus, and he is now a recognized leader in our church.

Some of us instinctively think of developing leaders all day, every day; others have to work hard to make it a priority. Before it will work for a team, though, the pastor has to be a consistent model.

Have Specific Plans the Week After the Second Conversation

I'm usually long on vision and strategy, but short on details. I did a pretty good job of training our staff to bring specific, detailed objectives after we laid out the plans for the second year, but I could have done better. After all, this is a crucial time in the three-year plan. At this point the team is transitioning from concept to application. They've spent a year learning and growing, and are preparing to put what they've learned into action.

I had told them to bring their plans for the second conversation, giving them a quick verbal list of what they should include. Most of them did a good job, but a few were still a bit unclear about what I was expecting. It required more time for them to identify and fill the holes in their plans. If I had it to do over again, I would have written a list on the board or sent an email with these exact specifications:

» The names of the five (to seven) people they had selected to equip;

» The four books and twelve messages for their teams;

» Their plan for when to discuss each of their books, the chapters they would cover at each meeting, and the person who would lead the discussion each time; and

» Their personal list of twelve books and fifty-two messages for the year.

The plan they submitted that day would chart their courses for the year, and I would hold them accountable for their progress at the end of the year. I may not have been quite as clear as I should have been the first week, but by the end of the next staff meeting, everybody had clear expectations.

Fight Against "Vision Drain"

For a year before the second conversation and throughout the second year, I communicated often and passionately that the culture of our church was changing. For us to grow, we couldn't simply work harder or add another program. We had to expand our capacity by developing additional competent, qualified leaders. In many churches the goal of leadership is to fill in slots on an organizational chart so that all the tasks will be accomplished. That had been true of our church for many years. We had to change that kind of thinking so that mentoring leaders would become the norm for our staff and for each person on their ministry teams.

Old habits, though, die hard. To create a new culture, we had to fight against "vision drain." When we turned the corner from learning to application, some of the people on our staff tended to slip back into old and comfortable—but unproductive—ways of leading. I talked to one who was tired of trying to delegate responsibility to people on his team. He told me, with a hint of disgust, "It would be a lot easier for me just to do it myself."

> When we turned the corner from learning to application, some of the people on our staff tended to slip back into old and comfortable—but unproductive—ways of leading.

He looked surprised when I responded, "Absolutely. There's no question it would be easier in the short run. But in the long run, you won't help that person become a leader. And that's our calling."

Others had a hard time finding balance in their team meetings between compelling discussions about the principles in a book and taking care of the administrative details of the ministry area. I told them, "Don't neglect leadership development. Find a way to get the work done, but make sure you focus on building people into leaders. This year, we're all about equipping them." I modeled my attempt at balance in our weekly staff meetings. We spent well over half our time talking about a chapter in a great book and how to apply the principles with our teams that week.

For some of our staff, the transition from worker to equipper was extremely difficult. They hadn't yet developed the skills of vision casting and delegation, so they didn't have people in place to carry the load. As they tried to develop those new skills and equip people, the still had to do the daily work of the ministry. During this transition they were doing two jobs: the old one because they hadn't yet equipped other people, and the new one of preparing them to serve. For a couple of months they were tired and frustrated, and they wondered if it was really worth it.

The previous year I had talked a lot about the vision and strategy for the three-year plan. Just a few weeks into the second year, I realized I needed to talk at least as much in the coming year to reinforce our current strategy. Again and again, I spent time in our staff meetings and during personal appointments energizing and encouraging staff members so they didn't drift back to empty checklists. I worked to enflame their vision so they didn't forget that their goal was to build a network of passionate multiplying disciples. I reminded them often of the benefits of leadership development: to them, to the people on their teams, to the church, and to the kingdom.

I didn't feel bad about having to remind them. I need to be reminded about a lot of things (just ask my wife, Jenni), and the Scriptures emphasize certain themes over and over again. Where do we find stories of redemption? From Genesis to Revelation. Why is it included so often and in so many different ways? Maybe because we're kind of dense and need so many reminders. I didn't get upset with my staff because they needed to be reminded where we were going. It was a good reminder for me, too.

During the first few months of the second year I tried to gauge the mood of each staff member. Most of the time I waited for people to come to me if they were having problems with the shift. In retrospect, I wish I had taken a bit more initiative to go to them, especially during those first couple of months, to ask how they were doing. Yet when we talked, we had wonderful conversations. Sometimes we discussed the difference between dumping a job on someone and delegating responsibility to that person. We talked about a wide variety of issues related to selection, communication, scheduling, and caring for the people on their teams. The period of adjustment lasted a month or two for the ones who were struggling, but they learned a lot in a brief time. With a little encouragement and a fresh perspective from time to time, all but one came through with flying colors.

> We needed a crisp, clear statement we could put in front of the people we lead all day, every day.

I took our staff away for a three-day midyear retreat to regroup and recalibrate our vision. During that time we created a new vision statement we could memorize and live by: "We're developing generations of Christian leaders for kingdom advancement." This statement wasn't for our weekly church program, but for us and the people on our ministry teams. We needed a crisp, clear statement we could put in front of the people we lead all day, every day. The goal of building multipliers was new to the people on our staff team, so we wanted to create an environment in which building multipliers was the core of the culture—so central that no one would think of building a church any other way.

But as I look back on that year, I realize that I didn't have to do all the vision casting. At least once a month in staff meetings I should have set aside a block of time for people to tell stories about how God was working in the lives of people on their teams. We did that to some extent, and when we did, it was fantastic. But we could have done it much more frequently. Everybody loves to hear stories about God at work and celebrate in response.

Train Staff to Motivate Volunteers

Throughout military history a clear distinction has existed between a conscripted army and a volunteer force. Conscripts fight because they have to. Some of them may develop a genuine desire to fight for a cause, but many are merely putting in their time. On the last day of their service, they're gone! Volunteer armies, though, fight because the individuals have chosen to be there. They joined the ranks because they care deeply about the cause, and they're willing to die to defend their homeland, family, friends, and rights.

If we misunderstand the nature of volunteers in our churches, we run the risk of missing out on their strong and lasting motivations. They want their lives to count, and they want to serve next to people they trust and respect. They aren't in it for money or prestige, so we can't threaten to withhold a paycheck if they don't perform well. But if we tap into their heart's desires, they will work, grow, and become their best for the greatest cause the world has ever known.

> We often make one of two mistakes as we lead volunteers: we demand too much or we expect too little.

We often make one of two mistakes as we lead volunteers: we demand too much or we expect too little. What they do with their time is up to them. They don't have to invest it at church. They could spend it in a hundred other ways, but they have chosen to serve God. If we expect too much from them, we almost always reveal our disappointment when they don't rise to meet our lofty demands. Nobody likes to feel condemned, so volunteers often drift away when they believe we have demanded too much from them. But the opposite mistake is just as problematic. Some of us are afraid to ask people to do much of anything. Perhaps we've been condemned or used by leaders in the past, and we're sure not going to do the same thing to our people! When we ask too little of them, they feel devalued and we fail to capture their hearts. As one leader said, "Small plans do not enflame the hearts of people!"

Jesus, of course, exemplified the right blend. He calls all of us, paid staff members and volunteers alike, to lay down our lives for Him—to demonstrate complete and abject commitment, holding nothing back. But He also invites us to join hands with Him. In this relationship, He assures us of His love, overlooks countless mistakes, forgives our selfishness, soothes our fears, and uses us to change the world.

Novelist Dorothy Sayers observed that Jesus experienced three great humiliations. The first was at His incarnation when He stepped out of the glory of heaven to become a baby. The second was at the cross where He took all the punishment we deserve for sin. The third, she says, was at Pentecost when Jesus gave the church custody of His reputation. We represent Him to the lost and broken people of the world.

It seems absurd that the Lord of glory would stoop so low as to entrust us be His hands and feet, to share His heart with others . . . but He has. When we realize the depth of His grace, we will ask people to give Him everything they have because He deserves nothing less. And then, just as He is patient with us, we need to be incredibly patient as they grow, falter, fail, and learn.

The question leaders need to repeatedly ask volunteers is: "How can I help you?" Part of equipping others is helping them find the right fit so they are thrilled to use the gifts God has given them. We need to equip leaders of ministry teams with heart and skills to motivate volunteers. As we model for them, our volunteers will share the same passion for Christ with the people they select and lead.

I have learned to ask my team a single question to galvanize this point. I ask, "What have you given your team this week that they can't get anywhere else?" It might be something tangible like a great book, a CD, a handwritten note, or a meal together. Or it might be intangible, but potentially as valuable as gold: affirmation that they are God's people doing God's work in God's way. We can look volunteers in the eye and tell them, "I'm so thankful to God for you! Your love for Christ and your care for people really encourage me." How often do they need to hear words like that? How often do *you* need to hear them?

Volunteers aren't just drawn to a cause. Often they are first attracted to a leader who exemplifies love for God and then is committed to the cause. One of the most important principles I can impart to my team (and they to their teams) is a clear grasp of how to motivate volunteers. It doesn't take long to discover that the hearts of paid staff are affected far more deeply by sincere personal attention than by any tangible threats or rewards. Heart motivation is the source of real change. Strategies and plans are important, but only if they are fueled by genuine passion for God and His people.

Change the Culture, Whatever It Takes

Leaders often underestimate the power of an entrenched set of values and behaviors—that's what culture is. Thank God, I wasn't under any illusions about what it would take to change the culture of our staff team and our church. From the beginning, I had been well aware that it would be a long, slow, tough climb to transform the hearts of our staff so that they saw themselves as multipliers instead of workers.

With the size of the task in mind, I charted a three-year plan. We outlined how we would build stairs for each staff member to get to the point where we could reach the goal and dunk the ball. I knew it wouldn't be enough to read one great book and have a few weeks of terrific conversations. We would have to read dozens of books, saturate our minds with scores of great messages, and talk about the shifts in attitude and actions until I was blue in the face. With the exception of the incident with Joel, I wasn't ever really frustrated.

It wasn't enough to have one or two ministries in the church on track with building multipliers. For the culture to change, all of us had

> It wasn't enough to have one or two ministries in the church on track with building multipliers. For the culture to change, all of us had to own the new vision.

to own the new vision. All of us had to learn to live and breathe multiplication. We had to learn to see it with new eyes when we read the Scriptures, hear it in our prayers (because they reflect what we think is really important), and impart it to the people we meet all day, every day. We couldn't just try out a new way of thinking and hope it stuck around a while. We had to bathe in it and let it permeate every cell in our bodies.

To change the culture of an organization, you have to be tenacious and patient. You need a detailed plan to inject new values into people's minds and hearts, and you need regular reinforcement of vision and celebration. But nothing changes the culture unless someone embodies positive change, eats and sleeps it every day, and is willing to sacrifice comfort in order for the change to happen. I simply couldn't let us keep going the way we were going. Changing our culture wasn't just a nice idea I dreamed up one day. God put fire in my bones. That's what it took for me, and I think that's what it takes for anybody who wants to make dramatic change in any organization.

I love when Bill Hybels of Willow Creek Community Church quotes the cartoon character Popeye. Whenever Popeye got really frustrated, he glared at the audience and growled, "That's all I can stand. I can't stands it no more!" That's how I felt as God first gave me a vision for the three conversations, and I had the same passion for change at the end of the second year. Leaders can't be satisfied with anything less.

A friend heard me speak on this subject, and he asked, "You say we reproduce who we are. What if in the second year I realize I'm only reproducing dull, rigid, lifeless people because that's who I am?"

"Then you repent," I answered him. "You listen to the Holy Spirit, and with a broken and contrite heart, you confess your sin of apathy, rigidity, demanding people perform, or whatever your sin is. Then you soak your soul in the grace of Jesus. Let His forgiveness cleanse you and make you whole. Ask Him to give you a tender heart for Him and for His people. And trust Him to give you a plan for leading your team. But before you roll out any plans, let the people around you know what God is doing in your life. People long to follow an authentic leader. Be that. First, be that."

The message of repentance isn't just for ineffective pastors or staff members. All of us have a long way to go. During that three-year process, I discovered deficiencies in myself and my leadership that I would never have seen if I had kept doing things the way they had always been done before. As God revealed my flaws, I confessed sin, admitted needs, and trusted Him to make me a better leader. And when those things came up in our discussions of leadership principles, I told our team how God had spoken to me through the Word or in prayer. I told them about things I had been wrestling with and how God wanted me to change. I shared how God was using the things we were learning in my heart, my relationship with Jenni and the boys, and my role as pastor.

> Maybe the most important trait I modeled to our staff was the continual desire to be a learner.

As I look back, maybe the most important trait I modeled to our staff was the continual desire to be a learner. I told them, "I am making a commitment to you to always keep learning and growing. I don't ever want you to look at me and think, *Scott's slacking off, so all this leadership development stuff isn't as important as he said it was.* I believe it's crucial, so I have to model a passion for personal growth in heart and skills. I promise that I'll keep growing at a pace that won't limit you."

We had phenomenal discussions prompted by the books we read. For example, when we read Jim Collins's *Good to Great*, we discussed the diagnostic questions he asks in the book: What are you best at doing? What are you passionate about? And what feeds your growth engine? I told them, "You know, whenever we have a great new idea, we try to add it to what we're already doing. As a result, we've become terribly unfocused, and it's killing us. What are the things we do best? What are we passionate about, and what drives our growth?"

We had one of the best conversations of the year around those questions. We even did some demographic research to study our area, discovering that 80 percent of the homes around us have children under eighteen years of age living there. We realized that we needed to pare back some of our activities so we could focus on three areas: leadership development, children, and students. (It would have been really disappointing if we hadn't made developing leaders one of our three top priorities, but they listed it first. Cool! We were making progress.)

I would have wasted my time trying to pull the wool over my team's eyes about my flaws. They could see them as well as (and maybe better than) I could. I admitted them, and we talked about the need for all of us to keep learning and growing.

The first of Martin Luther's 95 Theses that he tacked to the door of the church in Wittenberg was, "When our Lord and Master, Jesus Christ, said 'Repent,' He called for the entire life of believers to be one of repentance." We shouldn't be surprised when God shows us that we need to change. It's the way of life for anyone who is serious about following Jesus.

Work on Seeding and Sending

As we became more focused on leadership development as a core value of our team and our church, our discussions raised a lot of important points. In our efforts to build multipliers, we didn't want to lose sight of the two ends of the leadership pipeline: seeding and sending. Jesus came "to seek and to save the lost." Everything we are and everything we do must be aligned with the vision of the kingdom to invite people to step out of the domain of darkness into the kingdom of Christ. As we equip people to serve, we need to constantly ask:

»   How does this role, this task, or this event plant seeds of the gospel in people's lives?

» How are we expanding our fields so that we plant even more seeds?

» How well are we watering and fertilizing the seeds we plant so that we see genuine fruit in a harvest of new believers?

At the other end of the pipeline, we should be thrilled when we train people and they leave to serve somewhere else. I've heard pastors complain that they get frustrated because they pour time, energy, and resources into a staff member who then resigns to go serve at another church. Or staff members complain that they invest in key volunteers who decide to serve in a different ministry at the church, or who go elsewhere.

One pastor told me with a tone of disgust, "I'm done training staff members to become leaders. After I've poured my heart into them, they move to another town or leave to start a church. All my efforts are wasted." Such a viewpoint is baloney, and it's myopic. We're part of God's global kingdom, so we don't equip people just for our church.

> Whenever we train people to be multipliers, we hold them with an open hand. God is the one who decides where He wants believers to serve.

Whenever we train people to be multipliers, we hold them with an open hand. God is the one who decides where He wants believers to serve. If He leaves them with us, we'll be partners in the greatest challenge on the planet. If He moves them somewhere else, we ought to celebrate like crazy that He has called them to a different part of the field. We should send them off with gratitude for their work and for all God is going to do through them wherever they're going.

I'm happy to equip leaders. Some will stay with us and others will discern a calling somewhere else. The principle of sowing and reaping means that others sometimes will reap what we have sown, and we will sometimes reap what others have sown. No problem. I want to equip leaders to be the best they can be. Our staff members get calls from all over the country to join various church teams or plant new churches. I'm thrilled when they tell me about those invitations. It means we're building people with passion, whose gifts are being sharpened, and who are seeing God use them in incredible ways. Those invitations aren't a threat to me. They're compliments to our leadership development strategy.

Eliminate Organizational Enablement

Psychologists have identified one of the problems in dysfunctional families as "enabling." Enablers don't let others in the family experience the consequences of their bad behavior. Instead of letting someone fail and learn from his mistakes, enablers fill in the gaps, lie about the problem, and cover for the person, which perpetuates his bad behavior. Enablers define "love" as bailing people out instead of confronting the hard truth of laziness and rebellion.

It took me a long, long time, but I finally realized that I had been enabling Joel the whole time he had been on our staff team. I had excused his behavior. "Oh, that's just Joel," I would say. "Everybody loves him. He'll do better next time." But the truth is that people thought Joel was doing a good job because I was stepping in to clean up the messes before anybody could see the problem. I was like an overprotective, smothering parent repeatedly stepping in to fix a child's problems. I told myself time after time that I was helping him as an act of service to God—that I was "acting in love" and "believing the best." But it was foolishness. In reality, I just didn't want to have any hard conversations.

Confrontation would have been painful for both of us, so I excused his behavior again and again. And no, Joel didn't do better next time, even after I gave him an additional year to step up. At the end of the second year, I had to face the uncomfortable fact that we had two problems: Joel's irresponsibility and my enabling his behavior. I could call it "love" on my part, yet I wasn't willing to do the hard, right, loving thing—let him fail and learn from the consequences of his failure. I was as much a part of the problem as he was, and it was time to put an end to the organizational pathology.

Another mistake on my part was never saying anything about what was going on. I should never have let the problem go on so long without communicating with our board. By the time I told them, they were so shocked that I had to do damage control with them before I could talk to Joel and Kim about leaving the church. I had stored up the pain without sharing it with the people who were tasked by God to oversee the health of our church. Of course, I had rationalized it by telling myself that they didn't need to get involved, that it wasn't such a big deal anyway, and that Joel would surely change as we took steps toward becoming multipliers.

I ignored dozens of yellow and red flags during the first two years of our new strategy. As I look back now, I should have cleared out the fog from my brain, spoken more directly and much sooner with Joel, and informed the board much earlier so they could be part of the solution instead of becoming a major roadblock at a crucial moment.

I may be slow, but sooner or later, I learn. From that point onward, I made sure that I informed our board anytime I had a significant problem with a staff member. In fact, I have called special meetings of our board so I could tell them what was going on and ask them to pray. They asked

> Everybody benefits from a regular reporting schedule.

questions, and I answered every one. I wasn't going to be caught out on a shaky limb by myself again.

I also realized that I had been making too many assumptions in leading people. It wasn't that I was uninvolved with the team during those two years. We had wonderful discussions in staff meetings. In fact, Joel's participation made me believe that he was totally on board. And I certainly didn't want to institute rigid controls designed primarily for poorly performing people because rigidity feels oppressive to the overachievers.

However, everybody benefits from a regular reporting schedule. If I had designed one that was targeted and flexible, I could have used it to affirm and inspire the people who were doing well. I could also have implemented a more focused set of expectations for the one who was falling behind. I learned from this mistake, too.

Finally, Kim's response showed me that Joel had slanted things in his favor in their private conversations—if he had told her about our leadership development plans at all. I can imagine him telling her, "Honey, you won't believe what Scott's doing with our team!" Even if he told her about our new goals and plans, I'm sure he intimated that I was nuts.

If I had seen the warning signs (or if I had done something when I saw them rather than ignoring them), I could have asked Joel to bring Kim for lunch or coffee so we could talk together about the direction of the church. It could have been relaxed and informative, rather than the "come to Jesus" meeting we had after the second year. I could have helped Kim understand my heart so she didn't see me as she did in that fateful, tense meeting: with 666 engraved on my forehead. I had blown several leadership opportunities in my dealings with Joel, but I learned valuable lessons from each of them.

In spite of the explosive ending to the second year, it was a huge step forward for almost everybody on our team. Except for Joel, each person had turned a crucial corner. They had become the kind of models others wanted to follow, and they learned important lessons about selecting the right people and equipping them to pour themselves into others. We were ready for the third conversation, but before that could happen, I still had to clean up a mess.

Dan Celebrates at the
End of the Second Year

The principles I learned during the second year transformed my ability to lead people. The leadership development philosophy, strategy, and practice I use today are derived from the lessons of that year. Until then I had talked a good game about building leaders, but I had been a Lone Ranger. The people around me had functioned as helpers to make *me* more successful, and I liked it that way. During the year, however, I realized my God-given role was to make *them* successful. That may sound like a simplistic observation, but it was a game-changer for me.

As the year progressed, I was forced to deal with all the phony excuses I used to defend functioning as a Lone Ranger—a leader that Jim Collins describes in **Good to Great** as "a genius with a thousand helpers." I had to admit that I wanted people to see me as the genius, the hero, the indispensable key to success for our ministry. When I went out of town for a weekend, I was secretly glad when people said, "Dan, we almost fell apart without you. Man, we need you!" Now my desire to be perceived as the genius was changing. My goal was for them to thrive without me—and maybe not even notice when I was gone!

Another perspective that needed to be challenged was my "commitment to excellence." I was sure I could do every job better than anyone else. In many cases it was true, but only because I hadn't given others the training, resources, and experience they needed to do a great job. My pride had limited the growth of the people around me. It was time for that to change. I had to take a step back from self-sufficiency and see that equipping my leaders was my top priority in leadership.

For years I had talked about leadership development, but I didn't know how to do it. I thought that a front row seat to watch me was all anyone needed. The second year gave me knowledge and strategy to impart to people in my ministry area. Selecting the seven leaders and pouring my life into them happened because Scott created a structure and a culture that pressed us into new habits that created leaders. The books and messages weren't the key. They were just tools to stimulate rich interaction—one-on-one and with our leadership teams. Scott's process was moving me from a worker to an equipper, and then to a multiplier, and my role was to create a strategy and culture in our ministry area so every leader moved along the same path.

All the passages about leadership development and all the principles I'd heard at conferences finally were put into practice during the second year. I wondered how I could have missed it for so long, but I didn't beat myself up about being slow to catch on. At least I was getting the picture now.

Near the end of the year, I read my existing job description and realized it had been written for a worker. I decided to rewrite it to emphasize that my primary job was to equip leaders. (I suspected I would need to rewrite it again after the third year when I understood the principles of multiplication much better). I also revised the job descriptions of everyone reporting to me so their primary role was leadership development. The words on a page may not mean much sometimes, but for those of us in the student ministry, the new job descriptions were an important statement—to ourselves and to each other—about our vision for our roles as leaders. This change has become the new norm for all the staff members at The Oaks. A fourth of each person's time is devoted to selecting and training leaders who serve in their ministry areas.

Think about it . . .

1. Have you ever had a leader who asked you to do things he or she had not modeled? How did you respond? What impact did this leader have on you and others?

2. What are some causes of "vision drain"? Why is it inevitable? How can you minimize it in your ministry?

3. What are some important differences between conscripts and volunteers in an army? What are the parallels in churches? How have you seen volunteers motivated well?

4. Why are *seeding* and *sending* important features of a healthy leadership development strategy in a church?

5. How would you define and describe *enabling*? How have you seen enabling cause more problems than it solves in families and in churches?

6. If you had been leading Joel, how would you have handled the situation with him during those two years?

7. What are two or three of the most significant lessons you will need to implement in the second year?

Chapter 7

The Third Conversation: Grow!

The reward at the end of the second year, we decided, was a day of paintball. I left Joel in my office, quickly shifted into party mode, and before long I was covered in paint. That night we took our spouses out to dinner for some good Texas barbecue. Nobody even mentioned Joel. They knew he had come to the end of his rope on our team. As we sat around the table, Dave asked, "We're meeting next week to talk about the year, aren't we?"

I almost laughed. I knew he didn't think I had forgotten, so I told him what he wanted to hear me say: "It's on! You bet we are."

Brittany knew I wasn't going to spill the beans, but she asked anyway, "What's the plan for the year?"

I smiled. "Just show up and be ready."

"I can't wait," she said with a grin. "I'm so excited about where we're going this year. I've never had such quality leaders and such a clear plan to build into their lives." I could tell some of the others were surprised by her comment. They had presumed she didn't really need any of what we'd been talking about.

She saw their expressions, and she explained, "It's true. I had been coasting for a while, but now I have much clearer ideas about how to develop leaders for our ministry."

Dan said, "If we keep growing leaders like we've been doing, there's no telling what God's going to do!"

Richard remarked, "I've got to tell you, Scott, I wasn't too sure about this whole plan when we got started, but it's been remarkable, just remarkable. Even my Sunday school teachers are thinking about equipping people to teach, and they're forming teams to shepherd people in their classes. I never thought I'd see the day."

Mark caught my eye and said, "To be honest, I was pretty scared going into last year. I'd always focused on putting together a great band to perform well in our services, and I'd never—never—even thought about developing leaders in my role. I can tell you that this past year has been the best year of my life. It's been incredible to see people find roles, expand their vision, and form the other two bands. I don't ever want to go back to the way things used to be. Thanks, Scott. I really appreciate all you've done to make this happen."

"No problem." I noticed that Justin was quiet. He's always reflective, but something seemed different. I asked, "Hey, Justin, are you fired up about next year's plans?"

He smiled and said, "Oh yeah." But I could tell something wasn't quite right.

We got back to the church and piled out of the van and cars. I told the team, "Be locked and loaded for next week's staff meeting. It's going to be fun." But I knew I had some unfinished business to take care of before we met.

The next day I told Joel that I wanted to meet with him and Kim. And after the explosion, I met with the board to inform them of the developments. The next few days were a whirlwind, but we finalized the severance agreement. Joel turned in his letter of resignation, and we planned the party to send them off. That week I met with each staff member to fill them in on what was happening, and during the next two weeks I met with seventy-five other leaders in the church.

I was emotionally spent, and with everything else going on, I thought about postponing the third conversation with our team. I didn't want to lose momentum with them, though, so we met at our regular time the next week. I asked Rob, Joel's assistant, to step in as an interim director for media arts. I didn't know how long it would take to find the right person to replace Joel.

A Quick Recap

I'm glad I'd been thinking about this meeting for several weeks. I was certainly distracted by other matters, but when the team walked into my office, I was ready to go.

As soon as they sat down, I could sense the heaviness in the air. We were there to discuss the future, but first we needed to take some time to talk about the pain of losing Joel. I'd already met with each member of the staff individually, but new questions and doubts can arise pretty quickly.

I told them, "I feel sad about Joel. I know you do, too. I've asked Rob to join us and lead that department on an interim basis. I want to assure you—as I'm sure you already know—that I love Joel and Kim. I wanted him to be on our team, to be part of where God is taking us, but his heart wasn't in it. It wasn't my choice for Joel to leave our team. That was his choice. Is there anything you want to say? Anything you need to ask me about? I don't want to leave anything hanging in your minds as we move ahead with our plans."

I scanned their faces. Finally, Richard spoke for the group, "Scott, you were a lot more patient with him than I would have been. We're glad to have Rob with us this morning. Let's get going."

"Okay," I answered. That was what I needed to know, and I also wanted to prepare them for any questions people might ask. "If any of you is approached by people who have questions about Joel, you can explain that he realized his goals weren't in alignment with ours, and he wanted to find a place where he fit better. If someone isn't satisfied with that answer, please ask the person to call me. I'm going to talk to a lot of leaders in the church, and I'll be glad to talk to anyone else who is interested." That seemed to be enough about the past. It was time to talk about the future.

I had planned on giving a short review of the past two years that morning, but Rob hadn't been part of any previous discussions, and Joel hadn't filled him in much at all. So I took the time to review our entire analysis, vision, strategy, and plans. I wrote the number 650 on the whiteboard and explained that we kept falling back to that number every time we went up to 900. Beside the number I drew a bucket with holes in the side. Then I wrote the number 1,000 on the board with a basketball goal next to it. I explained that we weren't going to lower the goal to fit our capacity. Instead, we had created steps to help us reach our goal. I drew the steps reaching up toward the goal.

I wrote the words *worker, equipper,* and *multiplier,* and I said, "Two years ago, most of you were workers, but after a year, we didn't have any workers on our team. We all committed to equipping five people on our ministry teams. And this year, we're going to shift to multiplying. I explained again that everything we had done during the past two years was designed to move us toward becoming multipliers **(figure 6)**.

Rob was taking in a lot in a short period of time, but he seemed to be catching on. Unless I was sadly mistaken, he quickly grasped every point we were hurriedly covering.

I asked, "How do you think we are progressing in meeting our goal of 1,000?"

Figure 6

Mark said, "I can tell we're pretty close. We are, aren't we?"

"Right now, about 925 attend every week. Yep, we're close." I didn't want to lose the teachable moment, and I had just covered the whiteboard, so I connected the dots. I pointed to the bucket, and I asked, "We're not falling back. Do you know why?"

Dan said, "Yeah, because our holes have moved up!"

We all had a good laugh, but he was exactly right. "Precisely," I responded. "In the past year, each of you has developed greater capacity in your ministry area. You've poured your heart into at least five people, and those newly equipped volunteers are now leading others more effectively than ever. Pretty cool, huh?"

Justin asked, "But what about the problem with Joel? When this kind of thing happens, sometimes a lot of people leave."

"No doubt," I told him. "But two things are different this time. One is that you have built relationships with the people on your ministry teams. They trust you. They respect you. They aren't going to assume the worst about you, about me, or about the church when we go through a difficult time like this. And the second difference is that we're not trying to avoid the issue. We don't have to go into every detail about the past couple of years regarding Joel, but we can truthfully tell people that we all committed to a goal and a process, and when Joel realized he didn't fit, he chose to go somewhere else. Those two things will resolve a lot of doubts before they are ever uttered."

We were facing the biggest crisis of the past couple of years, but we were confronting it as a team. In the previous two years we had forged common goals through hundreds of great discussions. We trusted each other, and we were ready to defend God's leading for our team and our church. Principles that had been theory two years before were now established values and habits for our team.

"I'm so proud of you!" I almost shouted. "Do you know where we're going this year?"

Dan remarked, "You told us last year. You said we needed to pick the right five—people who had the capacity to lead five more."

"Exactly. At least three, and better, five."

Plans to Multiply

I erased a lot of the things I had written on the board, but I left the basketball goal, the number 1,000, and the steps. I was still reviewing, but I wanted to drive certain points home.

On the bottom step, I wrote "Modeling." I explained, "The first year, we focused on becoming good models for people. We asked, 'If people do what I do, care the way I care, and love the way I love, what kind of church would this be?'" Everyone was nodding like they had heard this a few dozen times before.

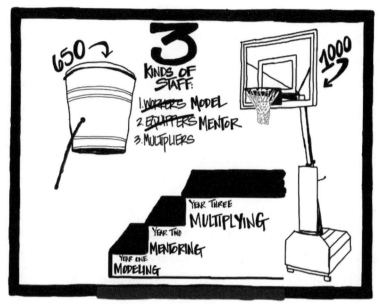

Figure 7

On the second step, I wrote "Mentoring." I told them, "Last year we were committed to selecting five to seven blue-chip people for our ministry teams so we could equip them, or mentor them, all year." They had heard that, too. "And this year, it's no surprise to you that we're going to concentrate on multiplying."

I wrote "Multiplying" on the third step **(figure 7)**. As Dan had said, we had talked about picking five people with the expressed goal that each of them would learn to lead five more.

I found enough space on the board to draw a spider diagram. I drew lines representing our team, each with five lines representing teams of five, and now, each of those with three to five lines representing new people being equipped for ministry. I asked, "So how many strong, godly leaders will we have at the end of this year? Let's do the math. Seven times five is thirty-five. Add to that the nine people on the church board whom I am working with, and the eight of us. That's a total of fifty-two leaders at the end of last year. Now if your thirty-five and my nine equip at least three leaders each . . . let's see, forty-four times three is 132. But if each leader equips five people instead of three, we will have 220 leaders. Two years ago, you were working with a few leaders in your ministry. Now, in two years, there are fifty-two strong leaders in the first and second generations. And a year from now when the third generation is complete, there will be between 132 and 220! And that's out of 900 to 950 people in the church. That's an incredible percentage of people involved in personal development. Awesome!"

I expected somebody to say something sarcastic at this point. Sure enough, Mark said, "Looks like a pyramid scheme to me."

I took the bait. "Yeah, but it's *God's* pyramid scheme." My comment was cheesy, but it was the best I could do at the moment.

I asked, "How did we form our plans last year? What questions did we ask as we selected people and equipped them?"

Brittany answered, "We asked *who*, *when*, and *how*?"

"And those are the questions each of your leaders needs to answer: '*Who* are the five people I can select who will have the capacity to lead others? *When* can we meet so that I have time to impart heart and train them in skills? And *how* will I shape the content so that it has the biggest impact?'"

As I turned again to 2 Timothy, I told them, "Remember, the process of leading leaders who lead more leaders never ends. We are raising up generations of multiplying leaders until Jesus comes back. Here's what Paul wrote to Timothy in the opening verses of 2 Timothy 2: 'You then, my son, be strong in the grace that is in Christ Jesus. And the things you have heard me say in the presence of many witnesses entrust to reliable men who will also be qualified to teach others.'"

I gave them a moment to reflect before continuing. "Now, let's talk about the *who, when,* and *how* of your team's teams. First, who will they select?"

A few of them were already ahead of the game. Richard told the group, "Well, each of my teachers has developed a team to oversee their classes."

"Great."

Brittany said, "I have a leadership team of women who each lead five ladies who shepherd the table leaders in our women's ministry."

"You're already there."

A Creative Approach

Most of the others on the team were still trying to figure out how to make multiplication work for them. They understood the concept. No problem there. But the nature of their ministries was quite different from Sunday school classes or the women's ministry.

Dan had more volunteers in the youth ministry than any other part of the church. "I'm a little confused," he said. "I've got seven people on my leadership team. It has been fantastic working with them. Several of them are working with teams of volunteers who meet with junior high and high school kids. We have a training meeting every Sunday for our leaders and volunteers, but we don't do it in layers or generations like you drew on the board."

"Got it." I understood exactly what he was talking about. "I'm not concerned about how clearly generations appear on a chart. I'm much more interested in your finding a system that works for your people and your ministry. The clean organizational structure seems to work really well for Brittany, but Dan, you've got a massive conglomeration of people, events, and needs. You might need a slightly different approach.

Let's do it this way for all the ministry teams: Either the individuals on your teams can identify three to five people to equip this year, or your ministry can create a regular training meeting where your team can equip a group of volunteers and identify potential leaders. That way, a team of five may end up working with fifteen people, or thirty people, or fifty people. Who knows?"

Dan added, "And at that meeting, people on my team can choose three to five people, give them attention, meet with them outside the training meeting, and help them find a great place to serve in our ministry."

"Perfect!" I was glad Dan saw the potential of connecting the two ideas. I tried to summarize: "The training meeting can become an ongoing filter for your ministry. New generations of leaders can use it to invite people, see if they catch the vision, begin to build relationships, and help them find the right fit where they can pour into kids' lives. Every leader in your ministry recruits people to come to the training, and there, they find out if they really fit. I like it."

Plans for the Third Year

I wanted to remind the team that quality produces quality. I told them, "Last year, we talked about the Negative One Differential Factor of Leadership. Do you remember that?" They nodded, but a couple of them looked like they needed a refresher course. "It means that we can attract and equip people no sharper than we are, and probably a notch or two lower."

I walked to the board and started drawing. "The first generation is our staff team, the second generation is your ministry teams, the third generation of leaders is the people they're equipping, and a fourth generation is their teams. If you and I are fives, we'll only be able to attract fours, and they'll attract threes, and they'll attract twos. Folks, we can't do much good for God and His kingdom if the folks who are making contact with people in our community and newcomers to our church are twos out of ten. That means the people in this room have to keep growing in love for God and keep sharpening our leadership skills until we are nines. That way, we'll attract much sharper people to join us, people who have huge hearts and a tremendous capacity to build more leaders." I paused for a second to let this sink it. "This means that you and I can't slack off in our commitment to learn and grow this year. It's no time to coast. In fact, it's never time to coast. We have to stay sharp to attract gifted potential leaders."

"So," I asked, "what should our plans be for reading books and listening to CDs this year?"

Mark said, "I think we can do at least what we did last year."

Dan chimed in, "Yeah, that sounds right to me, too."

Others were nodding. I wrote on the board as I said, "Okay, we're going to read twelve books and listen to fifty-two messages this year. How many are you going to ask your teams to do?"

Mark said, "Same as last year: We'll pick four books and twelve messages for them, and they can pick a wild card book of their own."

I looked around the room, then I asked, "And what are they going to ask their teams and training groups to do?"

Brittany remarked, "It seems reasonable to ask them to do the same thing. Five and twelve seems appropriate to me."

Everybody agreed, so I wrote that on the board. "Your task this year will change. Last year, you equipped people. This year, you'll be helping those people equip a new generation of leaders. They will need to select well, because you will tell your people that each of their folks needs to have a strong team at the end of the year. Last year, you gave me your plans of *who*, *when*, and *how*. This year people on your team will need to give you their plans of who they plan to pick for their teams, when they will meet with them, and the content they will use to equip them . . . the list of books and CDs."

Dave observed, "It's going to take me a while to explain all this to them and get their feedback. I don't think I can have it to you for our next staff meeting."

"Good point," I told him. "Can you talk with them and have it two weeks from now?"

"Yeah, I think that will be okay."

I looked around and it appeared that everyone else thought the plan would work. I told Rob, "I'd like to meet with you tomorrow to help you work up your plans. You're starting from scratch, but I think you can begin selecting a team fairly soon. Are you up for that?"

Rob replied confidently, "Sounds good to me."

Surprisingly, Rob didn't look like a deer caught in the headlights. He had been tracking with us during the whole conversation. He was two years behind, but he was catching up fast.

I tried to review everything we had said. "Okay, two weeks from now you're going to bring me your plans with the following elements: You'll have a list of twelve books and fifty-two messages for yourself, and it would probably be helpful if you email your list from last year to each other for ideas. For your ministry teams, you'll bring your plan for *who*, *when*, and *how*. It will contain the names of the five to seven people on your team and a list of the four books and twelve messages they will use. You'll also let me know when you plan to meet with them, which books you will cover with them, and who will lead the discussions. And finally, for their teams, you will meet with them and ask them to give you their plans for *who*, *when*, and *how*. Got it?"

Mark looked at me like, *You've got to be kidding. You expect me to remember all that?* The others were writing furiously. I told them, "I know this is a lot. Why don't I send you an email this afternoon with all this on it?" They seemed relieved.

I wanted to be sure they understood that the next couple of weeks were going to be pivotal. I told them, "These are going to be the most important meetings you'll have all year. They will chart the direction of everything you do with your teams. Make sure you do what I've done with you: Go over the reason we're focusing on leadership development; draw pictures; write *worker, equipper,* and *multiplier* on a whiteboard; and explain the plan. Be clear about the vision, ask them to follow your example, and let them know that the people they select will follow their example. Don't get too caught up in making a diagram work. Help your team members select well, and be creative in creating training events to filter new leaders if that fits your situation. Don't be surprised if it takes a while for them to catch on. Emphasize how God has used this process in your life. Communicate heart and vision as well as the specific plan. Any questions?"

> Help your team members select well, and be creative in creating training events to filter new leaders if that fits your situation.

Two years ago we had thrown a pebble of vision into our church's pond. The first ripples were small, but soon they spread to make a bigger circle. Now we were ready for the ripples to become much larger. I was really excited about how well my team had caught the vision so far. Already, I knew the ripples were expanding when I shared my heart with our staff. They told their ministry teams what we talked about, and they communicated with passion. It was a thrill for me to see people on their teams (whom I barely knew) talking about the things I had shared with our staff a week or two before.

The ripples kept expanding in generations of new leaders and the spread of concepts and heart to new ministry teams. In fact, as we finished talking about the principles flowing from our staff meetings to their ministry team meetings and then to the next level of meetings I had an idea. I thought I might end each staff meeting by asking, "Based on what we've talked about today, what needs to ripple through the leaders in your ministry area?" But it didn't sound like such a great idea when I told them about it. At the mention of "ripple," they jumped immediately into comments about me and cheap wine. They just don't appreciate the brilliance of some of my ideas.

Still, I was excited about the ripple effect. I thought about how the vision that began with eight of us would soon permeate 200 or so hearts. Some things that are vital to the church can be covered in a sermon to the entire congregation, but others need both a Sunday morning message and a personal touch—and some points are best left for heart-to-heart interaction of teams of likeminded people.

My staff made fun of me, but they understood the power of this method of connecting with our people. They were no longer observers sitting on the sidelines while I poured out my heart to the people in our church. They were vital channels of information and inspiration to every person in their ministry areas. In fact, our growth couldn't happen without them. They felt more connected than ever to the vision of the church.

Dave said what was on everybody's mind. "At the end of the year, if we meet our goals . . ."

I tried to pretend I didn't know what he was talking about, but I'm not too good at stifling a laugh. "Yeah, yeah. I almost forgot. When you make your report a year from now, if you do what you've said you will do, I'll hand you a check for $500 and we will party like mad!"

Richard said, "This is getting kind of expensive for the church, isn't it?"

"No way," I assured him. "It's the best investment our church has ever made. Look at the payoffs we have already seen, and we're just getting started. I assure you, the board sees this money as entirely worthwhile. So do I."

> It's always messy to implement a concept with real people with all kinds of hopes and fears —and the more people who are involved, the messier it can get.

Mark grinned, "If it's paying off so well, can we get more money?"

"No chance." What a smart aleck.

I was sure the third year would prove to be a challenge. It's always messy to implement a concept with real people with all kinds of hopes and fears—and the more people who are involved, the messier it can get. I was encouraged that Rob didn't die of a heart attack as he listened to us talk about expanding to a third generation of leaders. But Justin's quietness concerned me. Maybe he was upset about Joel. Maybe he was having a bad day.

I asked if anybody had any questions. They agreed to come to my office if they had any, so I prayed for us. I thanked God for this team of people who had proven their commitment to Him and to His kingdom. My heart was overwhelmed with gratitude for all God had done in us and through us in the past two years. I asked Him for wisdom now as each person planned to select the next generation of leaders at our church. I was excited about what God was going to do.

As everyone walked out of my office, Dan turned and said, "Scott, if all of us do what we're talking about today, our goal of 1,000 is nothing. We're almost there now, and we haven't even multiplied." He smiled, "You're going to have to reconsider your goals, bro."

Justin Was Catching Up

**Justin Lathrop was our Young Adults Pastor.
He currently serves as the Director of Strategic
Relations for the Assemblies of God.**

I had just joined the staff at The Oaks a few months before Scott had the first conversation and outlined the plan for us to become multipliers. I was a recent college graduate, so Scott had asked me to lead the ministry for young adults. Even though I was new to the church and the staff team, I was eager to dive in. The first two years were really challenging for me. It seemed like I was drinking from a fire hose, but I was learning incredible lessons. Even years later, I can remember the specific books and talks God used to change my life.

In the second year, I had picked five terrific volunteers, and they loved the reading and listening assignments. They devoured all the leadership principles and spiritual motivation. Every time we met, I felt even more energized by their excitement.

In the third conversation, Scott showed us the logical next step of having our five leaders identify a few more leaders—and do for them what Scott had done for us and we had done for our five. When we calculated the number of equipped, skilled, motivated leaders we would have at the end of the third year, we were really pumped! The strategy made perfect sense because broadening the leadership base would tap into more enthusiasm and more talent from additional people. When Mark said it looked like a pyramid scheme, we all laughed, but we realized it was the way God wanted the church to operate—not for financial profit, but to expand His kingdom.

To be honest, if Scott had stopped after the second year, I think I would have been content to remain an equipper. It was miles farther than I had been as a worker! The third year challenged us to dream bigger dreams, create broader strategies, and push ourselves to find more capacity to transform our own teams from workers to equippers. This year would be crucial to the growth of the church . . . and to our development as members of the staff team.

I was excited about the third year's strategy, but I quickly realized there wasn't an abundance of rising leaders among the young adults. It would be a stretch for my leaders to find three people to pour themselves into. I had plenty of questions about how it would play out in our ministry, but I was eager to give it a shot. We had seen God open plenty of doors in the first two years, and I was convinced He could do it again.

Think about it . . .

1. How did Scott try to diffuse the potential explosion of Joel's depar-
    ture from the team? What did he do well? What would you have
    done differently?

2. If there had been a "vision drain" in the second year, how much
    more could Scott and the team expect in the third year? What
    could they do about it?

3. What are the benefits and liabilities of being flexible about the
    form of selecting and equipping the third generation of leaders?

4. What was the message Scott was sending when he talked to his staff again about the Negative One Differential Factor?

5. What things could Scott have done to make the assignment for his staff even clearer?

Chapter 8

The Events of the Third Year: The Dark Side of Success

I had a lot on my mind in the two weeks after our third conversation. We were launching an exciting year, but my mind and my heart were still caught up in the difficulties with Joel.

We had the going-away party to celebrate Joel's and Kim's time with us, and people asked awkward questions. I tried not to eavesdrop as Joel was repeatedly asked, "Why are you and Kim leaving?" But I could clearly see that a number of people were confused and hurt when they heard his answer. I hoped he would remember his agreement to avoid condemning the church, but I knew that problems were inevitable in situations like this. I wanted to move on as soon as possible. I felt torn between the past and the future.

Clarifying Plans for the Year

I made sure to follow up on sending my staff a list of expectations for the year. The email contained all the elements of the strategy we had discussed, and I reminded them that this time they had two weeks to turn in their plans. Each staff member would submit:

» A list of twelve books and fifty-two messages for personal growth (They were to email last year's list to everybody on the team to give them ideas.)

» Plans for the five to seven people on their ministry team, including:

   Who—the names of the people

   When—the time set aside to meet with them

   How—the four books (with one more to be individually chosen) and twelve messages for them, the chapters to be covered in each ministry team meeting, and the person who would lead those discussions

Each person on all of the ministry teams would also be submitting a similar list to the person who was equipping him or her:

» Whom they had selected as their three to five key leaders (or in lieu of that, when they had scheduled a large training meeting where key leaders would select people to equip)

» When they would meet with their chosen team

» How they would equip *their* teams—the four books and twelve messages for the year, the chapters to be covered in each team meeting, and the person who will lead the discussions

I think the staff really appreciated the email with everything clearly spelled out for them. They seemed ready to go, and I was thankful for their enthusiasm.

Pleasant Surprises

During those two weeks I was meeting with the seventy-five or so church leaders to discuss Joel's leaving. A few of them were outraged at first, but most simply wanted to hear my explanation. I had seen churches split when the congregation took sides after someone was fired or had resigned, and I didn't want that to happen to us. My meetings with the board had been enlightening. I acknowledged my major mistake of not communicating the reality of the situation for over two years, and once they understood that, the shock wore off and they supported my decision. I also made sure they understood that the decision wasn't to fire Joel. When he realized he didn't fit any longer with the direction of our church and stopped working alongside the staff team, he had essentially resigned.

To be honest, I expected at least a few church leaders to be upset enough to either leave or stay angry for a long time—my estimate was 10 percent. My first surprise during those weeks was that *nobody* left, and to my knowledge, nobody became bitter toward me. After each meeting, I thanked God for His goodness.

A week and a half after the third conversation, I happened to be in my office (which was rare during those two weeks) when Rob stuck his head in the door. He asked, "Pastor Scott, can I talk to you a minute?"

I said, "Sure. Come on in."

"I don't want to take up too much of your time. I know you're busy," he said humbly. "But I have a question."

"No problem, Rob. Shoot."

He began, "I know I'm way behind everybody else, but I—I hope it's alright—asked five people in media arts to be on a team with me. They all said they would, so I hope that's okay with you."

I wanted to say, "Okay? You've done more in ten days than Joel did in two years!" Thankfully, I mustered up enough tact and grace to give him a huge hug instead. "Yeah, it's more than okay, Rob. That's the kind of leadership that this church needs."

"I wasn't sure where to start with them, but said that I would come up with a list of five books and twelve CDs for us to cover this year. They all said they were really excited about being part of the team. I forgot to explain the stuff about workers, equippers, and multipliers. Sorry about that. But I can tell them about that next time we meet."

"You've got plenty of time to explain all that to them," I told him. "I can't tell you how thrilled I am that you're taking initiative to build a team."

When I asked Rob to serve as interim director of media arts, I thought he might be just a placeholder until we found someone to take Joel's place. He had already shown that he was much more than that.

The Team's Reports

It had been a hectic two weeks, but I was feeling pretty good. I finally finished meeting with all the leaders about Joel and Kim, and those talks had gone so well that I felt like a ton had been lifted off my shoulders. I was convinced that our church wasn't going to go backward because Joel and Kim had left us. Joel was already looking for work in other churches. I sure hoped nobody asked me for a reference.

Then it was time for our staff meeting. The team came into my office to give their reports. The mood that morning was different. They were excited about our plans to multiply this year, but they knew it would require learning new skills and facing unforeseen challenges. But there was also a sense of relief. All last year they had known that one member of the team wasn't really on board. Joel hadn't verbalized his discontent, but everybody knew he was a flat tire on a racecar. Rob was already showing that he was part of our team, and everyone soon accepted him as one of us.

I never miss an opportunity to preach, especially when I feel excited about the direction we're going, so I took a few minutes to share my heart. I told them I was thrilled with how far we had come in two years, but that God was just starting to create a pervasive culture of passion among a host of rising leaders. We were seeing an amazing transformation! I was happy to be on a team with people who showed such courage and heart. They graciously listened, and then it was time for them to give their reports.

> God was just starting to create a pervasive culture of passion among a host of rising leaders.

One by one, they handed in their plans. They had worked really hard during those two weeks, meeting with their teams, sharing the vision for multiplication, helping people select wisely and find venues to equip them. I told them they needed to be creative in finding times and places that worked for each ministry area, and they did just that.

Brittany's second-generation leaders were meeting before the Bible study on Wednesday mornings with their teams of leaders. They had been doing that for a year, but she said, "Now we have more of a focus on equipping those women to be great leaders."

Richard told us that he planned to continue his monthly meetings with his Sunday school teachers, and that most of them wanted to meet with their class teams for an hour once a month to go over leadership principles, talk about specific applications, and pray together.

Mark had started two bands in the past year. Now both leaders were planning to gather their members monthly to equip them spiritually. They would still meet each week for practice, but once a month they would get together to go over chapters of books they were reading.

Dan had more people involved in his ministry than anyone else. People love to see young lives changed, so attracting volunteers has never been a problem for the youth ministry. He and his leadership team decided to go with the large training meeting. They suggested that everybody who was interested should attend church during the first hour and then go to the training meeting the second hour. (During the second hour, we had Sunday school classes for junior high and high school. Gifted teachers led those classes while all the volunteers attended the training meeting at the same time.) When everyone was together, Dan and his team planned to share their hearts, identify the skills people needed to work with junior high and high school students, and see who was ready to volunteer to join a team. Dan's leaders already met with teams of volunteers, but this meeting would allow them to cast a wide net, select the very best people, control the training curriculum, and keep their finger on the pulse of the youth ministry.

Dave implemented the ripple effect in the children's ministry. Each month he met with the directors of his departments to go through a chapter or two of a book to highlight principles they could use in shepherding children and volunteers. Then the next month, his directors used the same chapters and principles in meetings with their teams of volunteers.

Justin met with his leaders every month on Sunday night. They would have dinner together and he would equip them by having them discuss chapters of a book. Then each of the people on his team found a time, usually once a month, to meet with their teams for breakfast, coffee, or dinner and have the same conversation over leadership principles.

Everybody on the staff team found a way to make it work for the third generation of leaders they were equipping. Some of the second-generation leaders were going to meet weekly with their teams, and some met monthly. Some ministry areas were more administrative than others, but all of us realized that we could keep expanding the pool of competent, passionate leaders. Actually, if the church was going to grow, we didn't have any options. We had to expand our capacity to touch more lives.

Before we ended the staff meeting, Richard asked, "Pastor Scott, I'm not sure all of my teachers are going to have five people on their teams. I know that's our goal, but should I require that number?"

"Not at all," I assured him. "We shouldn't be worried about arbitrary numbers. What's important is that we're identifying the next generation of leaders, and we're pouring ourselves into them to equip them to serve God with all their hearts. Every ministry is different, so we have to be flexible in how we apply principles. In fact, you may have one class that needs a team of ten

> Every ministry is different, so we have to be flexible in how we apply principles.

and another that only needs two. That's entirely up to you. I trust each of you to figure out what works, which means you're going to have to trust God for wisdom for each of your leaders. Certainly, some things will be standard for each second-generation leader and each third-generation leader, but you'll have to determine how to define the standards and how much to flex."

"It would be a lot easier if you'd just tell me what to require of them," Richard said with a smile.

"Yeah, but you wouldn't have to trust God as much if I did that, would you?"

"I suppose not," he sighed.

Leaders in other churches may have come up with very different plans to equip the third generation of leaders, but I was happy with the plans our team devised. Volunteers are busy people. Their schedules don't allow them to be available all the time, so some flexibility and creativity is always required. Our team did a great job of finding a way to make it work in their various ministry areas. I was really proud of them. Of course, we would make some adjustments along the way, but at the end of this meeting we were excited about our plans for the year.

More Good News

About three months into the third year, I realized Rob had amazing leadership skills. Only a week or so after the staff reported on their plans, I met with Rob to discuss his new role. I told him that I believed the volunteers in media arts had pent-up energy and longed for someone to lead them. If he would encourage them, pray with them, ask for their input, listen to them, and share his heart when they talked about principles in the books they read, I was confident we would witness an explosion of passion for their work. I was wrong; it was a nuclear blast!

Only a few weeks later, I heard reports from his volunteers that thrilled my heart. They were talking about how God could use brochures, videos, and everything they produced to touch individuals, deepen the impact of every sermon, and reach more people in the community. I didn't know what Rob was doing with them, but I hoped he would never quit! The work they did on all their projects was exemplary. Joel had often needed my help to complete a task, but Rob and his team created new ways to add power to an event, a message, or a meeting. A new day had dawned in media arts.

It didn't take long for word to spread to the rest of the staff and the board that Rob had revolutionized his department—in his quiet and humble way. At a meeting, one board member suggested the obvious: "Why don't we offer Rob the permanent position on the staff?" The suggestion was unanimously approved, and I offered him the job the next day. He was blown away.

More good news arrived in a very different way. As Mark worked with his team, including the new bandleaders, they began pouring themselves into the singers and musicians, and God worked like He often does. People began confessing sins they had hidden for years. Some were sins of integrity, and some were sexual indiscretions. They cried together, extended forgiveness and assurance, and saw genuine changes in many lives. A marriage that was about to dissolve was restored by the grace of God. You can imagine how those experiences changed all the people on the teams. When they led worship, their hearts were more in tune with God's grace and power than ever before. Some of them wrote songs God had given them during times of prayer with their bands. It was a glorious thing to watch God work through Mark and his leaders.

I was reminded that real ministry gets past the surface in people's lives. When God touches hearts, all kinds of things become apparent: some wonderful and beautiful, others ugly and in need of redemption. Good leadership, though, provides an environment of love and authenticity. That's where people really grow.

Almost Ruined by Success

By the middle of the third year, God was doing amazing things on our ministry teams. People realized they had strengths they had never noticed before. Our second-generation leaders drank deeply of the confidence of the staff member leading them, and they, in turn, led their volunteers with passion and strength. Strong relationships were built, and people became proud of what God was doing in their ministry—*too* proud.

There's nothing wrong with noticing that God is at work through a group of people and being grateful for the privilege of being part of something special. But when success causes us to feel superior to others, or on the flip side, to feel jealous that others are more successful than we are, sin ruins the joy of seeing God at work. That's what happened to us.

The prophet Jeremiah wrote, "The heart is deceitful above all things and beyond cure. Who can understand it?" (Jer. 17:9) Instead of having hearts of humility and gratitude, some of our ministry teams displayed arrogance. Rather than supporting one another, we became competitors. When others seemed to get more attention, some of our people became bitter.

We had become a church of *silos*, a metaphor we sometimes use around the church. A business dictionary observes, accurately but wryly:

> "[Silos are] non-communication between departments, incompatible goal-setting, intra-company snobbery, or outright hostility. The term refers to the sealed-off nature of silos rather than to their utility in storing tomorrow's breakfast cereal. At its most extreme, siloing in the workplace leads to destructive competition among nominal allies while providing an opportunity to abuse agricultural metaphors."*

Some of the key volunteers in the youth ministry became so proud of their effectiveness and their esprit de corps that they looked down on people from other ministries. Critics called them "The Brat Pack" because they were so arrogant, but they reveled in the label. Leaders in the children's ministry were angry because some of their best volunteers left to work in the youth ministry. Some of the Sunday school teaching teams felt they had superior theology or stronger relationships than anywhere else in the church. I could go on and on.

Human nature is predictable. When one group feels condemned by another, those criticized seldom seek resolution through dialog. No.

---

* "Spirit Lexicon, Entry No. 78," *Spirit*, December 2009, 56.

They gossip and they accuse, and the wedge of distrust between the groups is driven deeper. I felt like our church had been transported to Corinth. People argued about whom they were loyal to, who had the best ministry, and how their team was better than anyone else's. I'm all for feeling good about what God is doing among us, but this was something different. It was rank, unvarnished sin.

I didn't see it coming, but when its ugly head surfaced, I realized I needed to help my staff learn to care more about the overall vision of the church than their individual ministries. We had spent over two years trying to create a new culture in each ministry, but I hadn't made sure we were together on the same bus. Our success became destructive, causing divisions and resentment. That had to change. As I prayed, God gave me two ideas to resolve the problem and help us learn important lessons: a ninety-day plan and a leadership retreat.

Silos are created when people on a leadership team have disconnected priorities, so I instituted a plan for our staff to have 90-day rolling goals every month. This may not seem to be much of a solution for arrogance, but I started with this plan to help our staff align with the vision for the church and with each other. Alignment, I was sure, would solve at least some of our problems.

> Silos are created when people on a leadership team have disconnected priorities.

I told our staff to work up a fairly detailed plan for 90 days, which would be updated every month. As a team we would talk about how to support each other and coordinate events for maximum impact. I asked them to write their top three priorities above the plans turned in.

For the first few months, one priority for everyone would be "humility and alignment with the overall goals of the church." I got the idea for implementing the 90-day goals from a leadership book called *The First 90 Days: Proven Strategies for Getting Up to Speed Faster and Smarter* (Michael Watkins, Boston: Harvard Business Review Press, 2003), which describes how the first ninety days at a job defines the trajectory of the person's employment. I adapted the concept to use as an ongoing planning tool to correct our trajectory. We had gotten off target when arrogance hijacked our success. It was time to get our act together again. I have always been stronger in casting vision than in management, but the circumstances required me to learn how to better manage our staff and their leaders.

When I introduced the 90-day plan, I told the staff, "I want to talk about where we are in our goals, strategies, and plans. We've seen God do some incredible things, but I want to be sure we have a quality that God considers really important: unity. Why do you think God values *unity*?" I wrote the word on the whiteboard.

Several of them offered ideas about how unity is crucial to families, ministry teams, and the church. Mark said, "The enemy loves division. That's one of the ways he gets us to take our eyes off Jesus. When we fight against each other, we're accomplishing his will, not Christ's."

I asked, "Has that happened to us?"

Nobody said a word. I said, "Let me read a passage of Scripture." I asked them to turn to Psalm 133. I read,

How good and pleasant it is
when brothers live together in unity!
It is like precious oil poured on the head,
running down on the beard,
running down on Aaron's beard,

down upon the collar of his robes.

It is as if the dew of Hermon

were falling on Mount Zion.

For there the LORD bestows his blessing,

even life forevermore.

I explained that when God's people are of one heart and one mind, it's like oil "running down" the beard and clothes of the priest. When we love God and each other with all our hearts, we experience God's anointing. His Spirit does incredible things in us and through us.

Unity among God's people is also like the dew on the mountain, nourishing everything that grows there. When we are in alignment, the Spirit of God causes people to grow in their love for Christ. Dew isn't dramatic, but it's consistent. Occasionally God drops fire from heaven to burn up an altar, an offering, and even water in the trenches as He did for Elijah. But more often, He gently refreshes us, redirects us, and gives us all we need to be the kind of people He called us to be. When we're unified around the love of Jesus, we just show up and God works to change lives.

> When we're unified around the love of Jesus, we just show up and God works to change lives.

The psalmist says that where the oil of anointing is poured and the dew falls, "there the LORD bestows his blessings." God withholds blessings when we compete with each other, when we resent each other, when we're envious and bitter toward one another, but He pours out His blessing when we are of one heart and mind. The enemy may try to curse us, but God commands blessing. We will experience temptations, but we can care enough about each other to notice when others are in need, to reach out to help, to pray, to encourage, and to stand in the gap by each other's side.

I asked again, "Have we seen this kind of unity among us lately?"

The Spirit had used His word to convict our hearts. Several people quietly shook their heads. One said, "No. My people have been proud and resentful." Others nodded. But one person felt defensive. He glared, "Okay, so we're supposed to be blindly unified around your vision for the church. Is that what this is about?"

"Not at all," I answered. "We have looked several times at the passage in Ephesians about equipping the saints for the work of service. A few verses later, Paul described our goal as equippers: 'Speaking the truth in love, we will in all things grow up into him who is the Head, that is, Christ. From him the whole body, joined and held together by every supporting ligament, grows and builds itself up in love, as each part does its work' (Eph. 4:15–16). I don't want you to be unified around me, and your teams aren't to be unified around you. The only One worthy of our complete loyalty and love is Christ, the Head of the church."

I guess my answer was acceptable. His glare faded, and he nodded to me. That morning God created in our team the prerequisite for change: a broken and contrite heart. It was the beginning of repentance.

I said, "Let's take some time to think and pray alone for a while. You can look at these passages or Philippians 2:1–5 or any others you want to read. I'll call us back in a little while, and we'll talk about how to achieve more unity and alignment."

We had a good time of prayer. When we came back together, I thanked God for each person. I thanked Him for forgiving our pride and resentment, and I asked Him to work deeply in us and our teams to create a spirit of Psalm 133 in our church. Then I introduced the 90-day rolling goals and explained how they would help us stay in alignment with God's calling for the church and with each other. It was a much-needed and worthwhile meeting.

I told them, "I'm going to meet with you individually each month to go over your plans. I want to know what you think are your top three priorities. I'll give you a hint: leadership development will always be one of the three. After I hear from you, I'll give you feedback to be sure you're in alignment with the overall plan. Then in our staff meeting, all of you will share your top priorities with each other. This way, we'll make sure we remain in alignment with each other."

We've been using that plan ever since, and it's been incredibly helpful. As people share their top three priorities with the team, they get immediate feedback, input, and buy-in from the others. To launch our plans each year, I tell them my top three priorities for the church, and we discuss how each ministry participates in each one. This simple planning tool has equipped us to become unified—of one heart and one mind—as well as in organizational alignment with each other.

Some people love to plan, but others would rather have their fingernails pulled out one by one. I have taught our staff team to ask two crucial questions when they plan: What are the biggest problems that need to be solved? And what are the biggest opportunities that promise progress and growth? Usually, the answers to these questions go a long way to shape their top three priorities and their plans, budget, and schedule.

Repentance is a beautiful thing in God's family. In a very short time, staff members who had been competing with each other became each other's biggest cheerleaders. Those who had resented one another now asked how they could help each other. Instead of each person responding only to me and not caring about each other, they established mutual respect, assistance, celebration, and accountability. We were becoming a team again, but a far stronger team than we had been before the divisions ripped us apart. It took a while for the spirit of unity to work its way through the generations of leaders at our church, and I wanted to do something to help that process along.

A few weeks after our "come to Jesus" staff meeting, we scheduled a Leadership Weekend. Our goal for this annual meeting was specific this year: we wanted to shatter silos.

Months before the meeting was scheduled, we formed six teams, each starting with a leadership team, a board member, a pastor, and a leader from each of the ministries. Each of those six groups was then given a list of sixty people from all the ministries in the church to recruit and round out their team. We intentionally mixed people up. Two months before the weekend, the sixty-six or so people on each team met to come up with a name and logo. Each team had been assigned a color to be reflected in their names, so teams became the Blue Bombers, the Green Hornets, the Yellow Jackets, and so on. A man in our church owns a t-shirt business, and we had shirts made for everyone with the team color, name, and logo.

When people showed up for the weekend, we had a crowd of 600—far more than the 200 or so on the organizational chart. Old men and little girls came with painted faces, crazy hats, and all kinds of paraphernalia. We held a talent show the first night, and people cheered like mad for the people from their teams. We had arm wrestling, a spelling bee, a domino contest, dodge ball, and all kinds of fun. The captains picked people to play in each game, and the others hooted and hollered for their teammates. We gave regular updates on the scores earned by each team. The teams sat together, so there were masses of each color around the room. People led cheers. They jumped and shouted each time somebody from their team did anything, like walking up to play a game. It was electric—like youth camp for adults.

We had a fantastic time together, but the weekend wasn't all fun and games. I taught on unity and leadership, and we prayed for every person at the event. I gave a talk about Psalm 133: "How blessed for brothers to dwell in unity." I shared my heart and my hope for our church. I said, "You may be a volunteer with youth or children or Sunday school or women's ministry or some other ministry of the church, and you think, 'Man, we have the best ministry in the world.' That's cool! It's good to be grateful to God for the people around you and the work you do for Him. But we're all part of a bigger whole. Every ministry of the church is crucial. In fact, Paul said that the ones who are weaker are actually indispensable, and those who don't get as much honor should receive special honor. So whenever we think our role is bigger or better than another, we dishonor God and

> Whenever we think our role is bigger or better than another, we dishonor God and the people who serve Him.

the people who serve Him. My friends, this grieves God's heart. This weekend we've had a lot of fun being the Blue Bombers and the Green Hornets. We've cheered for each other. Until we can cheer for each other's ministries in the same way—until we realize we are one body, one family under Christ—we're going to miss out on God's blessing."

I showed a clip from *Miracle*, the movie about the 1980 USA Olympic hockey team that shocked the world by winning the gold medal. In the clip, the coach Herb Brooks had the young men practicing weeks before the Olympics. He asked each one, "Who do you play for?" One by one, they give the names of their college teams. During a grueling workout, Brooks continued to ask the same question. Finally, when they were utterly exhausted, the players answered, "I play for the United States of America."

That's what Coach Brooks was waiting to hear. He told the exhausted young men, "Until you play for the name on the front of your jersey, you can't play on my team. That's all, gentlemen."

I told the group of 600 that day, "It's not bad that you're proud to volunteer and serve in a particular ministry. It's a good thing to love what you do—as long as you're even more proud to be part of the bigger body, the bigger vision of God's kingdom. Whose team do you care more about?"

I reached into a box next to me and pulled out a gray shirt that read, "Team Oaks Fellowship." I asked, "Are you willing to play for this team? If you're in, I want you to come down and get a shirt. Don't take the other one off. Just put this one on over it." I put mine on first.

It was an emotional moment. Some of the people in the room had been bitter rivals over the past few months because of silos in our church. Some had already repented because the staff had modeled a broken heart, but many still had some business to do with God. That afternoon, God touched their hearts. As far as I know, every person came down and put on a shirt. The variety of colors in the room all blended to gray. It was a visual demonstration that we had chosen to be of one heart in Christ. We

> This was a moment we could remember, like Joshua erecting a pile of rocks in the Jordan River to remind the people of God's grace in bringing them into the Promised Land.

sang a couple of songs together, and I was sure no one would ever forget that moment.

People will always be tempted by pride and envy, but this was a moment we could remember, like Joshua erecting a pile of rocks in the Jordan River to remind the people of God's grace in bringing them into the Promised Land. I'll never forget that day. I'm sure a lot of other people won't either.

Finding a Better Fit

After a couple of months of working on the 90-day goals, Justin asked if he could talk to me. He said, "God has put some pretty big things on my heart. I'm kind of scared about it, but I'd like to meet with you to talk about my future. I want you to know that I'm submitting myself to your leadership. I really want your input."

We'd been great friends for years, but his request seemed ominous. I'd been wondering for a few months what he was thinking, but I had no idea what he wanted to talk about. Was he going to resign? I carved out plenty of time to meet with him the next day because I was sure it was going to be an important conversation. He was doing everything in his role that anyone expected him to do. It wasn't a problem with rebellion or poor performance, yet I knew he wasn't fulfilled in his job. In addition, our staff had taken a psychological profile, and the scores indicated that Justin's engine was running at only half speed. I'd asked a counselor to meet with our staff to help each one tailor the job to talents and personality. The counselor told me that Justin might want to talk to me about his future.

He came in the next day, and the first words out of his mouth were, "Scott, I've been thinking and praying for a long time about my role, and I realize I don't fit. Since we've been doing these 90-day goals, it's become clear that there needs to be a change. I've enjoyed some parts of it, but I'm not the guy to lead the ministry to young adults. I've told you that I'm frustrated, but it's more than that. It's not the good kind of frustration that drives people to be more creative and productive. It's the kind that leads to depression. You need to find somebody else. I don't want to hang around and end up like Joel." Before I could offer a rebuttal, he continued, "But I have a plan. I know a guy who would be perfect for my job. Do you remember Paul? We interviewed him for a different position a few months ago."

I nodded, "Yeah, I remember him. I really liked him."

"I'd like to call him to come for an interview. And I want to give you a proposal for a new role for me." Justin handed me a few sheets of paper. When I glanced at it, I could tell it was carefully constructed. Without missing a beat, he continued, "I think I can do some things for our church that would be helpful. They're not even on the list of things you're planning for the future right now, but I hope you and the board will see value in them."

I looked more closely at the proposal. It described a position to pursue college accreditation for our Master's Commission leadership training program, oversee the marketing strategy of the program, organize the internship program connected to the training, and supervise the hiring and firing of staff—basically a human resources role. The funding for the position would come from the income into Master's Commission. Funding from government grants and an increase in student enrollment would more than pay for Justin's salary and expenses. From the tone of his voice and the thoroughness of his proposal, the only question was whether the board would see the value of the new position.

I only said, "Justin, I'm sorry you feel like you don't fit. I could tell something was bothering you. Thanks for telling me. I love your proposal, and I sure want to keep you here. I'll be happy to take it to the board." We spent the next hour talking about the person he was recommending to take his place and his vision for his new role. I told him how much he meant to me. Justin seemed relieved to have finally taken this step. I was relieved that he wanted to stay on our team.

For several reasons, I agreed that Justin's suggestion was the best possible plan for everybody concerned. The person Justin recommended to take his role with young adults was a super guy. I had met Paul a few months before, and I was really impressed with him. The role Justin proposed fit him perfectly, and if it worked, it would propel our Master's Commission program and our church to another level of effectiveness for the kingdom. I was instantly sold.

I had a productive conversation with the board about Justin's proposal, and they gladly agreed to shift his role. Paul came in for an interview, and we offered him the job. The transition from Justin to Paul took only a couple of months, and Justin instantly excelled in his new role. Master's Commission became The Oaks School of Leadership, with university accreditation and an infusion of federal funding. Enrollment has risen from 30 to over 110.

The change has proven to be even more helpful and fruitful than any of us would have dreamed. Justin was a good leader of the young adults, but he's an incredibly gifted and creative administrator at The Oaks School of Leadership where he oversees the hiring of staff. He has a gift of discernment, and many times his advice has saved us headaches and heartaches. He was always a valuable member of our team, but now he's more fulfilled and effective than ever.

Meeting the Goal

We had begun the year with about 925 people regularly attending our church, after growing from 650 in two years, and now we were so close to our goal that we could almost taste it. In the middle of the year, a board member handed me a slip of paper after the service one Sunday morning. I was talking with various people, but between conversations, I took a peek. It said simply, "1,000!"

> This time we weren't going to drain back down to 650. This time we had grown in our capacity to love and support 1,000 people.

In an instant, I thought back on the history of the church and all the times we had grown, only to fall back. The image of the bucket with holes in it flashed in my mind. This time we weren't going to drain back down to 650. This time we had grown in our capacity to love and support 1,000 people.

At the next staff meeting, we had a big party! Again, it wasn't the arbitrary number we were celebrating. Rather, God had given us a plan to increase our ability to care for more people. We had invested our hearts and resources in developing more and better leaders, and the number simply confirmed, "Good job!"

Besides, we saw God working in far more exciting ways. During those two and a half years, about sixty people sensed His call to go into vocational Christian ministry. We tried to equip people to serve God faithfully and well wherever they lived and worked, but we knew that He would tap some on the shoulder and invite them to go into ministry as a full-time vocation. And the thrilling thing was that many of those were people I hardly knew whom had been reached by the second and third generations of leaders in our church! I was more thrilled than you can imagine. Justin had helped a lot of those people discover their particular gifts and find places where they could serve the Lord. Pretty cool.

A Changed Culture

At the end of the year, I told our staff to be sure to come to the anniversary staff meeting with their reports. I reminded them of our goals and plans at the beginning of the year. I said, "Bring enough reports for everybody, but we're not going to discuss all the books and CDs and numbers. Come with one or two stories of how you've seen God work in people's lives as you've developed them as leaders."

On the day of our staff meeting, people came in with a heightened sense of excitement. Last year we'd had to deal with Joel's leaving, but that was ancient history. Paul and Rob were new to the team, but they fit right in. We weren't there to celebrate the culmination of a year's hard-won goals; we were partying because God had changed the culture of our team and our church. *We* had changed, and we would never be the same.

That morning they all handed out their reports, but to be honest, no one even glanced at them. We didn't need to. We were well aware what the others had done. The spirit of resentment that haunted us at midyear had been conquered by love, forgiveness, and respect. We went around the room telling stories of changed lives, second- and third-generation leaders who took leadership of a team of volunteers, strained marriages that were restored, prodigals who returned, and a dozen more stories of God's power—all because the ripple of grace kept moving out to touch more lives.

Dave looked around the room, took a deep breath, and said, "I can hardly believe who we have become." A couple of people said, "Amen," and the rest of us smiled.

I waited until the end to hand out the checks. It seemed anticlimactic, to be honest with you. They didn't seem to care about the monetary reward. Seeing leaders' lives changed was reward enough for all of us. At the end, I asked Mark to drive the van out to the front of the church. He grinned, "Are you going to be late again this year? Any difficult talks before you join us?"

I laughed. "No. Let's go."

We jumped in the van. Nobody hollered, but we all realized that we had changed in the past three years. It was a really fun day together. I wouldn't have bet on that a few months before, but God's grace is amazing.

Justin's Change of Direction

During the three years, one of the biggest changes in our culture of leadership happened in Scott's life. He became more patient, more focused, and more of a shepherd of our staff team. He also brought us some incredibly valuable resources. In the third year, he invited us to meet with a counselor once a month, and he had us take a battery of assessments, including the comprehensive California Psychological Inventory. All of us benefited. Those instruments helped us clarify our strengths and understand areas where we needed help. When Scott first talked about the assessment tools, I had no idea how God would use them to change the trajectory of my life and my career.

The counselor was a safe, objective, supportive person who allowed me to process all I was seeing from the assessments. Before long, I realized my gifts, interests, and strengths were pointing in a different direction from my role as pastor of young adults. Suddenly, I felt very conflicted. Great things were happening throughout the church and in our ministry. God had prepared us for a season of harvest, and I sure didn't want to miss it. It wasn't time to get off the bus!

The counselor and I spent a lot of time together. It was obvious that something needed to change. He said he would be happy to talk to Scott and begin the conversation among the three of us. He told Scott that my CPI showed I had a lot of ability that wasn't being utilized in my role, and he encouraged Scott to think creatively about my future. He told Scott, "Justin has some ideas about changing his role. He's going to come to you soon. Be sure to listen carefully to all he has to say." The counselor didn't want to rush things. He asked Scott for a couple of months so he could work with me and figure out what was in my future.

I loved what was happening on the team and at the church, but for a long time, I'd had a nagging sense that my role wasn't quite right for me. Thankfully, Scott cared about me and believed in me enough to help me find a better fit.

Since I had been at The Oaks, I had been most fulfilled when I could connect people with resources. When I saw people get the help they needed, I felt tremendously satisfied. The counselor and I worked on a plan to change my job description to be a church-wide networker, and in fact, soon I was helping leaders outside our church.

Paul explained to the Ephesians, "For we are God's workmanship, created in Christ Jesus to do good works, which God prepared in advance for us to do" (Eph. 2:10). I'd finally found the place and role God had prepared for me. If we hadn't gone through those years of learning to be multipliers, and if Scott hadn't provided such valuable resources of a counselor and the assessments, I probably wouldn't have discovered and pursued this role. I'm extremely grateful to God, to the counselor, and to Scott.

Think about it . . .

1. How would you have made sure the plans to multiply—developing the third generation of leaders—were crystal clear to the staff? What are some possible signs that your plans might not be clear?

2. What are the benefits and liabilities of being flexible in the implementation of leadership development the farther you go down the generations?

3. Have you ever seen silos in an organization? How did they affect people? How was the problem addressed (if at all)?

4. How well did Scott handle the problem of silos? What did he do well? What would you have done differently?

5. How did the 90-day plans help the staff get in alignment with the church's plans and each other?

6. What principles can we draw from Justin's realization that he didn't fit in his role and from his request for a job change?

7. How do you think Scott felt during the celebration staff meeting at the end of the year? What price did he pay to get there?

Chapter 9

Lessons Learned the Third Year: Changing the Culture

W ow, what a year! I thought we would face a few challenges as the ripple of impact continued out to the third generation of leaders at our church, but I had no idea we would encounter such enormous threats to our church. All of us on staff learned important lessons during the year. By the time we faced the problem with silos, pride, and resentment, most of us had completely forgotten about the difficulty of Joel leaving us at the beginning of the year. The lessons, though, start there.

Make No Assumptions

Every pastor and staff member of every church have heard horror stories of "terminations gone wrong." In many cases, misunderstanding and miscommunication lead to unresolved tension that lingers for months, if not years, in the hearts of the remaining staff and loyal volunteers. In the worst cases, churches must deal with bitter splits.

At the end of the second year when Joel told us that he hadn't fulfilled his responsibilities—again—my thoughts raced to the "what ifs." What if our church split over his leaving? What if I backed down and let him stay? What if I failed to communicate adequately with the church over what was going to happen? At that time I had no idea there would be such a problem with Kim, and I didn't dream that the board would question my judgment. I only had whatever nightmares are called in the daytime—the horror of what might happen if things went wrong.

My meeting with the board showed that I had failed miserably in my responsibility of keeping them informed. The issues with Joel had been building for four years, but for all they knew, the problem might have cropped up in the past week or so. It took a while to help them finally understand, and I haven't made the mistake of keeping them in the dark since then.

The day our team went out to celebrate, I had a lot of fun with them, but I was also thinking hard about how to keep the situation with Joel from blowing up. I asked God for wisdom. At some point during the day, the idea hit me that I could substantially diffuse the problem by meeting one-on-one or in small groups with the leaders of the church. I could explain that Joel resigned because he didn't fit any longer, listen to them, and answer any questions.

Many of the people I wanted to meet with had official titles in the church, but some were leaders by influence more than position. Over the next couple of days, I wrote out a list that came to about seventy-five people, not including our board members. I met with them any time they were available—for breakfast, coffee, lunch, dinner, tea in the afternoon, on Saturday morning, or Sunday after church. It didn't matter how crazy my schedule became. Wetting the burning fuse was my top priority. It proved to be a very effective strategy. I could tell that some of the people I met with were suspicious. They had heard stories of staff members being victimized by a demanding pastor, and they wondered if that was the case here. When I was able to share my heart, my love for

Joel and Kim, and my hope that God would lead them somewhere they could thrive, those meetings built trust instead of letting it erode.

The written severance agreement between Joel and the church is a standard procedure, and even though it was fair to both parties, he wasn't happy about it. He didn't appear to acknowledge that his refusal to fulfill his commitments to the team meant anything at all. He had been a good friend for a long time, and I had tried hard (too hard) to make it work for him. Attending the party to celebrate his service and say goodbye was awkward for me, but I put on a smile.

I think I handled the situation pretty well from the day when he said he hadn't fulfilled his responsibilities to the day he left, but I had failed to address the problem effectively the year before. I had also avoided telling the board the hard truth—probably because I thought it reflected badly on me. I made some changes in my leadership at that point so the problem wouldn't happen again.

Increasing Flexibility

I'm sure there are benefits to a highly structured model of leadership development in the third generation (and some might think we were too highly structured), but I wanted to push decision-making and creativity down the pipeline as far as possible. Some elements, of course, have to be consistent throughout the generations. For example, the requirement of reading books and listening to messages is standard operating procedure. But it's not appropriate or helpful for me to make all the decisions about the implementation of equipping the next generation. If people don't own the process, they don't learn important lessons of leadership.

The structure of different ministries varied widely. Dave's leaders in children's ministry have different needs and schedules than the volunteers in Dan's youth ministry. I continued to be the voice of vision and the process of developing multipliers, but I let each staff member, and then each ministry team member, select their people and figure out how best to equip them.

Last year I might have just let things take their course after leaders chose how they would equip the next generation, but this year I learned that I needed to manage things a little better (maybe a lot better). Regular reports, especially as we implemented the 90-day plans, kept me informed and kept leaders accountable. Those conversations invited dialogue so I could ask questions and they could ask for input on sticky situations. Flexibility proved to be an important aspect of our process, as long as we had a workable feedback loop.

Don't Let Success Kill You

The biggest shock of the year was the problem we had with silos in our church. The term doesn't adequately convey the severity of the problem. Arrogance ruins individuals' hearts and their relationships. It seems, however, that relationships are growing stronger because groups become allied against everyone else. Arrogance-based alliances are little more than gangs. Does that sound too harsh? Maybe you've never seen silos in action.

I first thought the sarcastic comments were part of young leaders feeling good about what God was doing through them, much the way guys talk when they're playing sports. I was watching as the third generation of leaders was being equipped. It was thrilling! Sure, they were ragging on each other. People often do that in a good-natured way. What could possibly be wrong with it?

I finally realized the problem was more than playful sarcasm— much more. People were being deeply hurt, and resentment had replaced gratitude and affirmation. By the time I saw what was really happening, it had become a cancer that threatened to kill all God had done to build leaders in our church.

> By the time I saw what was really happening, it had become a cancer that threatened to kill all God had done to build leaders in our church.

God gave me direction from His Word, and He gave me a conviction that the cancer had to be decisively cut out. But even as I talked to our staff about the principles from Psalm 133 and Ephesians 4, I knew that only God could create clean hearts. I could share my heart and God's Word, but the Holy Spirit had to produce hearts of repentance.

I knew that one meeting with our staff team wasn't going to fix the problem. I had to get more involved in managing our staff and their leadership development. I couldn't count on my ability to cast vision to keep us on track. I wanted to get us aligned with God's purposes again by implementing a systematic and organizational plan. To make sure our staff team was in alignment with the church and each other, we inaugurated the 90-day planning process. That way, each month we had a clear check and balance.

The process promised to be helpful to all of us, but there were still some residual elements of the cancer throughout our church. The Leadership Weekend was designed to address the problem of silos in a dramatic, visible way. It was monumental. I can't tell you how much fun we had, but when we all put on those gray shirts, God gave us a visual image of unity in His body. We have continued to have annual Leadership Weekends—no more shirts, but plenty of vision, fun, and unity.

I'm not so naïve to think that we'll never face the problems of arrogance and resentment again. We are redeemed people, but until we see Jesus, we're going to struggle with our old natures. Paul reminds us, "You were taught . . . to put off your old self, which is being corrupted by its deceitful desires; to be made new in the attitude of your minds; and to put on the new self, created to be like God in true righteousness and holiness" (Eph. 4:22–24). We forget his advice at our peril.

Adding New Staff

When Rob and Paul joined our team during the third year, I didn't ask them to go back to the goals of the first year. If they had needed to learn how to model a life of passion and skills, we wouldn't have hired them. They came and dove in where we were. Rob had to catch up by selecting a team and equipping them before they could select their own teams to equip, but his learning curve was incredibly short. The speed at which he caught on showed me that the volunteers in media arts were ready to go. They just needed a leader to believe in them, build into them, and give them an opportunity to fly. Rob had been working under Joel for over a year, but I hadn't seen any of his potential until he became the interim director of this ministry. Poor leadership had held him back. Now he was engaged, dedicated, and incredibly effective in building generations of leaders—in media arts of all places!

When Paul came on board in the middle of the third year, we knew we had a winner. In the interview process when we talked about the direction of our church in building multipliers, his eyes lit up like a kid on Christmas morning. I didn't have to convince him that it was a good plan for our church. He was all over it. I was also impressed that he spoke well of Justin during the transition. Sometimes people who are new to a role try to make themselves look good by denigrating the previous leader. Paul didn't do that at all. He had quite the opposite heart from our folks who had been creating silos. Paul was grateful for all Justin had done to build a strong foundation, and he thanked him openly, sincerely, and frequently.

Our vision and strategy for leadership development changed everything about how we hire people at our church. The bar was now set much higher. A lot of nice people want to work on a church staff, and many are excellent at performing tasks in the ministry. But that was no longer what we looked for. With the vision God gave us to multiply, we couldn't afford to hire workers, and we couldn't even afford to settle for equippers. We needed men and women with the capacity to build generations of multiplying leaders. The capacity of church staff determines where the holes are in our bucket, and we want to keep pushing those holes higher and higher. Many who teach the art and science of hiring staff talk about the importance of character, competency, and chemistry. I believe capacity is just as important if the person is going to fit into the plans God has given us to keep expanding His kingdom through building multipliers.

Our church doesn't hire leaders with the capacity to lead people at our current level of growth. As a benchmark, I look for people who can lead at twice the current capacity. How do we find people like that? I have learned to leave the hiring up to others who are more skilled in that area. To be perfectly honest, I stink at interviewing and selecting new staff. I'm pretty good

> Our church doesn't hire leaders with the capacity to lead people at our current level of growth. As a benchmark, I look for people who can lead at twice the current capacity.

as a visionary and a pastor, but those traits seem to make me less than shrewd in picking new people for our staff. I believe everybody can be terrific. Naïve? Yes, I'm afraid so.

Years ago I was the first (and sometimes the only) person to interview a prospective staff member. I would share my heart and my vision for our church, and if the person's eyes didn't glaze over, he or she was in! After a few mistakes, I realized we had people on our team who are outstanding at interviewing prospective new hires. They have a sixth sense to discern people's hearts, how well they would fit with our team, and how much capacity they can handle. Justin is one of those people. He has been incredibly valuable in his new role as a filter in hiring staff.

Now we take prospective new staff members through a couple of interviews and an extensive personality profile. In our conversations we talk about their personal development plans. If they don't have one, it's a red flag. We talk about their philosophy and process of equipping leaders and helping them multiply. Finally, our interviewers tell them stories about the three years we transformed our staff team from workers to multipliers. They tell every applicant, "Hey, you've got to understand. Leadership development isn't an option to Scott. It's a core value." Only after all those things check out do they send the person to me.

At that point, I can't mess it up. Jenni and I take the applicant and his or her spouse out to dinner to get to know them. I flame about what God wants to do in and through our church to reach the world. It doesn't matter that I don't pick up on some of the crucial elements of character, competency, chemistry, and capacity. The previous interviews, profile, and reference checks have told me all I need to know. All I'm looking for at that point is a green light from the Spirit. Thank God for people with the gift of discernment!

When new staff members come to our offices the first day, we already have a nameplate on the door, a computer on their desk, keys in hand to give them, and a note from me welcoming them to our team. I meet with them that day to go over their first 90-day plans and make sure they're in alignment with the church's goals and the rest of the team. I want each person to dive in at the point where the rest of us have struggled to arrive—nothing less.

The Person Who Has to Grow the Most Is Me

When we began three years before, I was soaking in all kinds of leadership principles from books, conferences, and CDs, and I was ready to roll with a plan God gave me for our staff. I knew I needed to stay ahead of people on the team in order to be a model for them, but I didn't realize how much I needed to learn during those three years. Moving our staff from workers to multipliers forced me to develop skills I didn't realize I needed. I learned to identify the subtle signals of laziness or rebellion much sooner. I learned to manage a growing ministry more successfully by implementing a planning system. And I had to confront a strong root of pride that formed because we had been so successful. Through all of these challenges, I had to depend on God more than ever.

In the third year, I felt like I was getting in over my head. I looked around for help, and God led me to a Dr. Samuel R. Chand, a man of unusual insight who agreed to mentor me. I have some wonderful friends in the ministry with whom I meet and share ideas, but Dr. Chand isn't in my life to make me feel good. He's there to push, pull, prod, and get the best out of me. He gives me assignments and holds me accountable. He's a terrific listener, and he distills what he hears me saying so that I understand myself even better!

My relationship with Dr. Chand has helped me in three concrete ways. First, I have someone to talk to who doesn't have an agenda. I don't have to wonder if he's going to take what I say and possibly use it against me sometime in the future. When I'm with him, his agenda is me, my heart, and my growth. He provides authentic encouragement, and I don't have to wonder if there are strings attached. When he says, "Scott, I'm concerned that you're too focused on this, and you're not giving enough attention to that," I know he's helping me see things more clearly without chiding me. Before I met Dr. Chand, I had no idea how much I needed honest feedback from someone I implicitly trust. It's incredibly valuable.

> I had no idea how much I needed honest feedback from someone I implicitly trust. It's incredibly valuable.

Second, he pushes me far beyond anything I could have accomplished on my own. Without him, I would have settled too soon at a lower level of leadership excellence. It's like this: I play racquetball. Years ago, I thought I was pretty good because I beat all my friends all the time. I entered a tournament that had A, B, and C brackets based on skill levels. I thought I could do well in the A bracket, but I entered the B bracket so I would be sure to win. Imagine my dismay when I came in fifth out of ten players. If I had entered the A bracket, I probably wouldn't have scored a point! Before I had the opportunity to see my racquetball skill in light of others, I thought I was hot stuff.

In the same way, Dr. Chand helps me see that I still have plenty to learn about leadership. Humility isn't always pleasant, but it's necessary for growth. Reading books and listening to messages add to my knowledge, but Dr. Chand stretches my brain and my heart so that my spiritual and mental capacity grow. Great mentors ask great questions. Dr. Chand asks questions that challenge me and sometimes haunt me. He looks into my soul and exposes fears and desires I didn't even know were there.

One time we were talking about a staff member, and he asked, "Which is more important to you, your friendship with that person or his contribution to the Kingdom?" I started to answer, but he interrupted. "Not now," he said. "Think about it and we'll talk next month." I would have answered quickly (and probably superficially), but instead I got to enjoy an enlightening month of thinking, praying, and wrestling with my response.

The third way Dr. Chand has helped me is through his seemingly endless list of great contacts. When I am struggling with something, he often says, "I know somebody who can help you." Many times he's been of tremendous value to me or our church because he's given me a name and a phone number.

Reflections

Before we began our three conversations, our church had vacillated between 650 and 900 for several years. By the middle of the third year, we hit our goal of 1,000 in attendance because the capacity of our leaders had grown so much. But we didn't stop there. In the next two years, we doubled the size of our church. Of course, we've had plenty of struggles as we keep building generations of leaders, but the ripples just get bigger and bigger.

The process we used to build multipliers isn't magic, and it's not mechanical. Any success in leadership development requires a divine factor. We can't force people to grow spiritually or the church to increase in size. We can plant and we can water, but God causes the growth. They are His people, and it is His church. It's our role as leaders to build the fireplace, but only God can send the fire.

The biblical mandate is to make disciples, to equip them for the work of service, and to find a Timothy who will teach faithful men and women who will then teach others. Paul described the essence of spiritual life in his letter to the Philippians. In response to God's grace, we want to please Him, and we work like crazy "with fear and trembling, for it is God who works in you to will and to act according to his good purpose" (Phil. 2:12–13). It takes all three ingredients to change lives: purified motives, hard work, and the supernatural power of God's Spirit.

We can't infuse spiritual life into the people on the staff team, the ministry teams, and the volunteers, but we can walk in obedience to God, model truth and grace, and invite people to join us in the greatest adventure the world has ever known. If we become the people God wants us to be, we can count on Him to command His blessing in us, in our teams, and in our churches.

Justin's New Role and New Vision

When the decision was made for me to change roles, the transition happened really quickly. Within weeks I had a new job description, and a new pastor for young adults was knocking on the door. I was now even more excited about our staff being multipliers because I believed God could use me to provide resources for their ministries.

My role wasn't only to provide excellent sources of curricula, books, and ideas. Perhaps my greatest contribution to the people on our team was to connect them with outstanding leaders throughout the country. Being a switchboard of relationships is second nature to me, and I was thrilled to see God use me again and again. It wasn't that I hated being the pastor of young adults at our church. I loved the people in our ministry, and I loved the people on our staff team, but I simply didn't fit the role where I had been serving. After the change, every day was like a glorious spring morning! I felt alive and useful.

I hope other pastors will give their team members the same resources Scott gave us. The counselor was a wonderful sounding board, and the assessments gave us accurate pictures of our abilities and interests. Some staff members fail to thrive because they're resistant and adversarial, but others struggle simply because they're square pegs in round holes. For them, the problem isn't sin and rebellion; it's finding a better fit.

I hope pastors won't overlook their staff as they shepherd people in their congregations. They need to love the people on their staff teams enough to listen to them, and then help them tailor their roles to maximize their talents and passions. If necessary, pastors can help them find a more appropriate role, and then celebrate their new direction with them.

When I think of our staff team, I can see incredible growth in each person who went through the three conversations. Those years combined the rigors of boot camp, the academic emphasis of graduate classes, and the practical application of an engineer. We lost one member of the team because he wasn't committed to the process, but the rest of us grew in monumental ways and are more effective today because we internalized the lessons we learned.

I would say two people gained more than anyone else: Scott and me. Scott has always been a dynamic leader, but the three years forced him to grow in his ministry philosophy, his patience with the process of change, and his shepherding skills. He's a better leader and a better man as a result of those three years. I'm glad Scott saw me as a valuable person, not just a cog in his ministry machine. When I realized I didn't quite fit my role, he didn't toss me aside. He loved me enough to help me find a place where I could thrive. In the third year, I found my true passion and calling. I can't explain how much this means to me. I'll always be grateful for the opportunity to live, love, and serve on Scott's team.

Think about it . . .

1. What are some benefits and costs of meeting with influential people when you need to diffuse a potential "bomb"?

2. What do you think is the right blend of standard expectations and flexibility for each generation of leaders?

3. What are the first signs of silos in a church? What are some effective ways you might respond to them?

4. How did the leadership development plan affect the way Scott's church hired staff? How might it affect your hiring procedures?

5. What are some ways Scott grew in his leadership capacity and skills during the three years? What might have been the consequences if he hadn't grown and if he hadn't found a mentor?

6. What have you learned as you've gone through this book? Is the concept of the three conversations a workable (and adaptable) plan for you and your church? Why or why not?

7. What are the next steps for you?

About the Author

Scott Wilson has been in full-time pastoral ministry for more than twenty years. He is the Senior Pastor of The Oaks Fellowship located in Dallas, Texas—now ministering to nearly 3,000 people each week.

Dozens of pastors and leaders have been strengthened to fulfill their destiny and dreams through Scott Wilson Consulting. The organization comes alongside church and marketplace leaders to enable them to achieve the full potential of what God has called them to do. Scott is also the Managing Director of MinistryCoach.tv, an innovative online platform for coaching pastors.

Along with his father, Dr. Tom Wilson, Scott helped start one of the most innovative public school systems in Texas. Life School currently educates 4,200 students in five locations in the Dallas area. In August of 2013 Life School plans to open its sixth campus.

Because of Scott's desire to train kingdom leaders, The Oaks partnered with Southwestern Assemblies of God University to create The Oaks School of Leadership, a specialized ministry training school within the College of Bible and Church Ministries at SAGU. Through this intense training program, hundreds of students have been educated, prepared for ministry, and sent out as harvest workers.

Scott is the author of several books. His latest release, *Act Normal: Moving Compassion from Niche to Norm,* is a daily devotional through the book of Acts. Scott's previous titles include *The Next Level: A Message of Hope for Hard Times* and *Steering Through Chaos: Mapping a Clear Direction in the Midst of Transition and Change.*

Scott and his wife, Jenni, have three boys: Dillon, Hunter, and Dakota. The Wilsons live in the Dallas area.

Resources

Throughout this book, I've mentioned planning guides and lists of books and audios. To download these and other resources, go to www.ReadySetGrowBook.com

» A 90-day planning guide

» A suggested reading list of outstanding books on leadership

» Sources for messages on audio

» Recommendations of pastoral and executive coaches

» Information about The Oaks School of Leadership

» Other leadership development tools

To Order More Copies

To order more copies of this book, go to www.MyHealthyChurch.com